DESMOND FORRISTAL

THE MAN IN THE MIDDLE

ST LAURENCE O'TOOLE
PATRON SAINT OF DUBLIN

VERITAS

First published 1988 by
Veritas Publications
7–8 Lower Abbey Street
Dublin 1
publications@veritas.ie
www.veritas.ie

This edition published 2013

ISBN 978 1 84730 434 6

10 9 8 7 6 5 4 3 2 1

A catalogue record for this book is available from the British Library.

Cover design by Colette Dower, Veritas Publications
Icon of St Laurence O'Toole written by Mihai Cucu. Commissioned
by the Archdiocese of Dublin for the Year of Faith 2012–13.
Copyright © Archdiocese of Dublin. Used with permission.
Printed in the Republic of Ireland by Gemini International, Dublin

CONTENTS

INTRODUCTION

'I have loved justice and hated iniquity; therefore I die in exile.' Those were the famous last words of Pope Gregory VII as he lay dying in Salerno in the year 1085. They could just as well have been spoken by Laurence O'Toole, Archbishop of Dublin, on his death-bed in Normandy in the year 1180. He too was a lover of justice and a hater of iniquity. He too died in exile, prevented by an arrogant and peevish tyrant from returning to the city and the country he loved so well.

For Dublin and for Ireland, his death was a tragedy. The one man who could make sense of the turmoil was gone. The peacemaker, the mediator, the man in the middle, who was respected by all sides, trusted by all sides, and indeed loved by all sides, had been taken away. There was no-one left who could bind up the bleeding wounds of the Irish people.

His own dying words lamented an opportunity forever lost. In his delirium he cried out in Irish, to the bewilderment of the French monks standing at his bedside. 'Alas, you foolish and senseless people,' he said, 'what will you do now? Who will cure your grievances? Who will be your healer?'

Yet there is one way in which his death in exile is a cause for gratitude. If he died in Ireland, we would know little about him today. A few scattered references in the chronicles and annals of the time would preserve the memory of a much loved pastor, but we would know nothing of the details of his life. In that age of violence and destruction, the Irish had little time or inclination for the writing of books.

France, on the other hand, was entering into the greatest century of its civilisation. It was during this century that the French were to lead the world in education, philosophy, music, art and architecture. The monks of the monastery of Eu were part of that new movement and they knew that their own greatest contribution would be to tell the story of the man who had died and been buried in their midst. It was a labour of love for them to collect all the information they could about his life and times and to set it down in writing for future generations to read.

They questioned the many Irish pilgrims who came to visit the holy man's tomb. These included his nephew, Abbot Thomas of Glendalough, his friends the Bishops of Ferns, Cork and Louth, and his successor, Archbishop John Comyn of Dublin, all of them willing and able to fill in the Irish background. They wrote to Ireland for details of his life and virtues and miracles, which were duly sent to Eu. They added their own eye-witness accounts of many wonderful cures that had taken place among sick people praying at the archbishop's tomb. They brought all this material to Rome and eventually in 1225 were rewarded by the canonisation of St Laurence O'Toole.

Most of our knowledge about him today comes from the various Lives of the saint written or commissioned by the monks at Eu. They were written in Latin and widely circulated. Copies of them are to be found in libraries throughout Europe. Within the last ten years Maurice F. Roche has identified and edited four different Lives, which depend on one another to some extent though each makes its own special contribution to our knowledge about the saint. I am deeply indebted to Dr Roche for making copies of these Lives available to me, together with much valuable background material which he has assembled. My thanks are due also to Fr John Meagher, Fr Benignus Millet, Mr Joseph Long and Fr Tom Stack for help with published material.

One other source needs to be mentioned. Gerald of Wales, often known by the Latin version of his name, Giraldus Cambrensis, was a Norman cleric and a younger contemporary of Laurence. He wrote two famous books about Ireland within ten years of Laurence's death. They are written from the Norman viewpoint and present a very unflattering picture of the Irish. They are gossipy, prejudiced, credulous, infuriating, highly readable and totally indispensable.

CHAPTER ONE

HOSTAGE

Laurence O'Toole was born near Castledermot in County Kildare, probably in the year 1128. His father was Maurice O'Toole, king of the district known as Hy Murray, which took in the southern part of County Kildare and the western part of County Wicklow. His mother was Dervail O'Byrne, a member of an important family in the area. A memorial stone in Mullaghcreelan Wood, some three miles from Castledermot, marks the traditional site of the O'Toole stronghold and the birthplace of the saint.

His father decided to call the baby Conor, a name which had been borne by many members of the O'Toole family. He sent him to Kildare to be baptised, which was a journey of some twenty miles from Castledermot. There were two good reasons for the journey. In the first place, it was desirable that the baby should be baptised by the Bishop of Kildare, since baptism by an ordinary priest was hardly fitting for the son of such distinguished parents. In the second place, it was an opportunity of making a goodwill gesture towards Donagh O'Connor, King of Offaly, who ruled over Kildare and had been at loggerheads with the O'Tooles for some time. The baby was to be reared in Donagh's household as a sign of good relations between the two chieftains. This kind of fosterage was a common custom among ruling families in those days.

On the road to Kildare, a strange incident happened. The group bringing the baby were stopped by a seer, a man who was reputed to have the power of prophecy. He asked them where they were going and why. They answered with the respect always shown in Ireland towards seers and poets and told him they were bringing the son of the King of Hy Murray to be baptised in Kildare and to be fostered by King Donagh as a pledge of peace.

'What name are you going to give the boy?' the seer asked. 'Conor,' they answered.

The man was immediately seized by the prophetic spirit and under its influence began to declaim a verse over the baby.

> This child shall be magnificent on earth
> and glorious in heaven.
> He shall rule over many, both rich and poor,
> and by the name of Laurence I order him to be called.

Though suitably impressed, the baby's escort found themselves in something of a quandary. 'We dare not ignore his father's instructions,' they said. 'That is not the name he told us to give to the boy.'

The seer answered, 'This very night I will go to his father's court and make sure that no blame attaches to you for the change of name.'

Satisfied by this promise, they continued on their journey to Kildare where King Donagh was awaiting their arrival. The baby was brought to the Bishop of Kildare who agreed to baptise him by the name of Laurence. The king then took him to his home, where he was treated with all the care and honour which were his due.

It is not easy to judge the meaning of the change of name. Some of the old writers explained it by saying that the name Laurence comes from the word laurel. They pointed out that the laurel is an evergreen plant and that this could stand for Laurence's evergreen faith. Furthermore, the laurel wreath is the traditional award for the winner of a race, and so it could stand for the heavenly reward which Laurence was to merit by his outstanding goodness and holiness.

These ingenious speculations are undermined by the fact that the baby was not baptised by the name Laurence but by the Irish name Lorcán. It was common in those times to latinise an Irish name by choosing some Latin name which vaguely resembled it. Thus Laurence's father was not really called Maurice but Muirchertach. Laurence himself used the name Laurentius (Laurence) when signing documents but was normally known in Ireland as Lorcán ua Tuathail.

The name Lorcán seems to derive from the Irish word *lorc*, which means fierce or cruel or savage. As such it would be a suitable name for a great warrior or military leader, but a singularly unsuitable one for a churchman who was to be distinguished for gentleness and charity and the quest for peace. Its only application could be in reference to Laurence's courage and determination in defending the rights of his people against the Norman invaders.

There is also the possibility that the seer was simply wrong. Many of the wandering bards of the time made a comfortable living from their poems and prophecies. People offered them gifts and hospitality for fear of being cursed or made the subject of a satirical poem. Some of them were little better than confidence tricksters, whose prophetic trances owned more to opportunism than to inspiration. Laurence's seer may have decided that a chieftain would like to think of his son becoming a famous warrior. No doubt he was well rewarded for his prophecy when he made his appearance at Maurice's court and told his tale.

❧ ❧ ❧

Laurence's early childhood was a happy and uneventful one. We are not told how long he remained with the King of Offaly before returning to his father's home, but he was evidently well treated in both places. His education was of the kind normally given to the sons of princes, which is to say he scarcely received any education at all. It was not considered necessary for a prince to be able to read or write. As long as he could ride a horse and wield a sword, he had all the qualifications needed in order to be an effective ruler.

Irish chieftains of that period lived by the sword and few of them died peacefully in their beds. It was an age of constant warfare. The ancient annals describe the year 1145, when Laurence was seventeen, in the memorable words, 'great war in this year, so that Ireland was a trembling sod'. The description could apply equally well to almost any year of his early life. The whole country shook to the tread of marching armies and the clash of sword against sword.

The main reason for the turmoil was the absence of any central authority. The country was a patchwork of major and minor kingdoms. Any chief could call himself a king, and most of them did. Maurice O'Toole was known as the King of Hy Murray, though by European standards he ranked no higher than an earl or a count. Over these minor chiefs were the kings of the five provinces, Leinster, Munster, Connacht, Ulster and Meath – though the size, shape, names and number of these provinces tended to vary from time to time. By European standards they would have ranked as dukes. Over the kings of the provinces was the High King of Ireland, who should have been able to provide the country with unity and authority. It was his inability to do so that led to the incessant warfare of the time.

The reason for this was that the high kingship was not hereditary. The high king was one of the provincial kings who by force of arms compelled the other provincial kings to recognise his authority. As long as he lived, he had to fight constant battles to maintain his position. As soon as he died, war broke out among the provincial kings to see who would succeed him. The lesser kings too used to fight among themselves, each trying to increase his territory at the expense of his neighbour, and often rebelling against the king of the province. Scarcely a month went by without somebody marching to attack somebody else. The rare intervals of peace resulted more from exhaustion than from goodwill.

Laurence was just ten years old when he found himself caught up in the brutal world of Irish politics. Hy Murray was regarded as part of the province of Leinster, which at that time was ruled by King Dermot McMurrough, the man who will be remembered for ever for having brought the English into Ireland. Dermot was still a comparatively young man, about twenty-eight years of age, but he had ruled Leinster since the age of sixteen and had already earned a reputation throughout Ireland for violence and treachery. Gerald of Wales gives a justly famous description of Dermot in his book *The Conquest of Ireland*.

> Dermot was a man tall in stature and heavily built, warlike and daring among his people, his voice hoarse from constant and continual shouting in battle. He preferred to be feared by all rather than to be loved. He was an oppressor of the nobles, an advancer of the base-born, an enemy of his own people and an object of hate to outsiders. All men's hands were against him, and he was against all men.

At the same time, he was not without attractive qualities. As a ruler, he was effective if brutal. As a warlord, he was recklessly courageous. He had great gifts of leadership and could command unquestioning loyalty from his followers. He was capable of acts of generosity, not least towards the Church, and was responsible for founding and endowing a number of monasteries and convents.

Dermot was an intensely ambitious man, who was determined sooner or later to make himself High King of Ireland. He was quite prepared to fight every king in the country if that was the only way to reach the crown. But before he could attack the high king and the other provincial kings, he had to make sure of the support of the chieftains of his own province of Leinster. In keeping with his character, he treated them as enemies to be terrorised rather than as friends to be won.

So it came about that Maurice O'Toole received a demand from Dermot to send one of his sons to him as a hostage. If he failed to do this, Dermot threatened to attack and lay waste the territory of Hy Murray. Maurice had little choice but to obey. He decided to send Laurence, the youngest of his four sons.

Being a hostage at the court of King Dermot was very different from being a foster-child with the King of Offaly. A hostage was a pledge for the good behaviour of whoever he represented. If Maurice acted in any way against Dermot's interest, he knew that his son would be made to suffer by being killed or mutilated. A very frequent way of taking revenge on hostages was by putting out their eyes, a barbarous practice that was widespread not only in Ireland but throughout Europe.

It must have been with a heavy heart that Maurice saw his young son leaving Castledermot for the court of the King of Leinster. The boy himself must have been even more downcast at leaving his home for such an uncertain future. Though he did not know it, he would never live in Castledermot again. There were, however, a few grains of comfort in the situation. One was that Maurice had no intention of doing anything hostile to Dermot and so there was no reason why any harm should come to his son. The other was that Laurence, as the son of a king, was entitled to live in the royal residence and to be treated with the same respect as one of Dermot's own sons.

≈ ≈ ≈

The King of Leinster's court was at Ferns in what is now County Wexford. The traditional residence of an Irish chieftain was built of wood and surrounded by wooden palisades and earthworks. This was not good enough for the restless and ambitious Dermot, and he imported builders from England to build one of the first stone castles in Ireland. The ruined castle still to be seen in Ferns is thought to be somewhat later than Dermot's castle, but it almost certainly stands on the same site and may incorporate part of the original structure.

This massive and rather gloomy building was the place where Laurence expected to spend his years as a hostage. Dermot had other plans for him. In defiance of all laws and customs, he ordered Laurence to be sent in chains to a remote and rocky area and to be kept there under strict surveillance. Here he found himself living in conditions worse than those of the poorest peasants, ill-housed, ill-clothed and ill-fed. One of the old writers describes him in these words:

> The noble youth had the spirit of a man in the body of a boy. But after spending some time there and suffering the scarcity of food, the biting cold of the strong north wind, and various forms of ill-treatment, this pleasing and good-looking boy was reduced to a sad bodily condition, starving, emaciated, his skin covered with sores.

The writer does not tell us where this ordeal took place. But there is a local tradition which claims that Laurence spent his exile in the Glen of Imaal on the south-western side of the Wicklow Mountains. It is a remote and secluded valley, surrounded by some of Ireland's highest mountains, and would appear to have been a very suitable place for Dermot's purpose. Some modern historians have cast doubts on this, on the grounds that the Glen of Imaal was not part of Dermot's territory; but the boundaries between one territory and another were vague and fluctuating and it is difficult to be precise about them after the passing of so many centuries.

Writing in 1928, Fr Benedict ODC described some of the traditional stories about Laurence that he found in the Glen of Imaal. At a place called Brittas in the northern part of the valley, there was a large field known as Laurence's field. It had once been surrounded by a belt of ash trees, whose remains were still visible. This is the place where Laurence was believed to have spent his exile. Nearby was a house which was known locally as Laurence's Castle.

Presumably there were some men assigned to the duty of guarding him and making sure that he did not escape. The local stories also mentioned a woman, who was among those looking after him and who was gradually won over by his gentleness and innocence. She was the only one among those around him who showed any compassion or affection for the boy.

❦ ❦ ❦

Maurice O'Toole soon became aware of the fact that his son was not living in the royal residence or receiving the treatment that was his due. He may not have known exactly where he was or what was happening to him, but he must have had a good idea that things were not going well. There was little he could do to help. If he attempted any kind of rescue operation, he knew the boy would probably be killed or blinded before the rescuers could reach him. But he never gave up hope that some turn of events would enable him to get the upper hand over Dermot and bring his son home again.

Two years passed before an opportunity presented itself. By great good fortune, he managed to take a group of Dermot's soldiers by surprise and to capture twelve of them. They may have entered his territory to steal cattle and fallen into a trap. At all events, their capture suddenly put him in a very strong position for bargaining with the King of Leinster. He sent word to Dermot that he had twelve of his men in his power and that he would put all twelve of them to death unless Laurence was set free at once and allowed to return home.

Dermot summoned a council of his advisers to discuss the unwelcome news. It was clear that a military solution was not possible. The O'Toole territory was too well defended for that. But Dermot was reluctant to release the hostage, as it would deprive him of his hold over Maurice and cause him to lose face among the other rulers. Was Maurice bluffing? Would he carry out his threat and kill the men, knowing that if he did so his own son would meet the same fate?

After careful consideration, the councillors advised him to let Laurence go. 'Twelve men are worth more than one boy,' they said. 'The strong are worth more than the weak, the healthy are worth more than the neglected and disease-ridden.' Dermot finally yielded and agreed to the exchange.

An exchange of hostages is rarely a simple operation and this exchange was more complicated than most. Maurice did not trust Dermot and Dermot did not trust anybody. Eventually a formula was worked out, using the Bishop of Glendalough as mediator. Maurice was to send the twelve soldiers to the monastery in Glendalough and Dermot was to send Laurence. As soon as Laurence had arrived safely, the twelve soldiers would be allowed back to Ferns and Laurence could go home to Castledermot.

In this unexpected way Laurence's two-year ordeal came to an end and he left the Glen of Imaal for the monastery of Glendalough. It is a long and round-about journey by the modern road, but no more than five or six hours' walk across the hills, going through some of Ireland's most rugged and beautiful scenery, passing by Table Mountain into Glenmalure and then crossing the saddle between Lugduff and Mullacor that leads down to the site of the ancient monastery.

According to local tradition, Laurence's joy at leaving the Glen of Imaal was not shared by the woman who had been looking after him. It is said that she was so heartbroken that she used to climb the trees and watch the paths across the mountains, in the hope that she would see him coming back again. Some of the old people could even remember a few lines of the lament she is supposed to have sung as she mourned for her lost little saint.

CHAPTER TWO

MONK

F rom a distance, the valley of Glendalough looked much
the same in Laurence's day as it does in our own. The
long upper lake, cradled between high cliffs and fed by
the Glenealo River, tumbling down in a series of small
cascades from the high plateau beyond. The lower lake,
smaller and less daunting, where the valley widens and the
ground begins to level out. The cathedral, the churches and
the high crosses scattered lavishly around the lakes and along
the banks of the river. The magnificent round tower, over a
hundred feet from the ground to the tip of its conical cap, a
reminder of the time when the monks needed a place of
refuge from the Viking invaders.

As he came closer, Laurence could see the smaller houses
and huts that have now vanished. The churches and the round
tower were built of stone. The residences of the monks and
students and other dependents of the monastery were made
of timber or of clay and wattle. He had never before seen so
many houses or so many people in the same place. The Irish
did not live in towns and the only centres of population in the
country, apart from the Viking settlements, were the great
monasteries. These were centres of sanctity and spirituality,
education and scholarship, art and agriculture. The great
monasteries preserved and fostered everything that was good

in Irish civilisation, and none of them was greater than Glendalough.

For twelve days Laurence wandered entranced through the valley of the two lakes. He was received with open arms by the bishop, who decided that he needed a few days of rest and recuperation before returning to his father. The bishop entrusted him to his chaplain, a kindly priest who took Laurence into his own house, fed him, washed him, clothed him, tended his sores and generally acted as both mother and father to the twelve-year old waif. He also attended to Laurence's spiritual well-being. We are told that he instructed him in the Lord's Prayer and the Creed. This need not mean, as some have thought, that Laurence did not know the two most fundamental prayers of the Christian faith. More likely, it means that the chaplain instructed the boy in the essentials of Christian living and belief, using these two great prayers as a framework.

At the same time, Laurence was breathing in the atmosphere and history of the monastery of St Kevin. It had been founded somewhere around the year 570 when the saint fled into the heart of the Wicklow Mountains to escape the disciples who were thronging around him and preventing him from praying. He came to Glendalough (which means the valley of the two lakes) and at the foot of the cliffs overhanging the upper lake he found a small level space which could be reached only by boat. Here he built a hermitage, hoping to find at last complete solitude. But even here his disciples eventually found him out. There was nowhere left to flee to, so he bowed to the inevitable and allowed them to form a community around him. When the original site proved too small for the growing numbers, they moved to a new place at the east end of the upper lake, where the ruins of St Kevin's Cell and Reefert Church still stand. After Kevin's death, the community continued to grow and they had to move to a still larger site to the east of the lower lake, now marked by the round tower and the remains of the cathedral and other churches.

The monastery that Laurence saw was almost six hundred years old and had grown steadily in fame and influence through the centuries. It had been richly endowed by kings and chieftains and its lands stretched far beyond the boundaries of the valley. These lands were carefully cultivated by the monks to provide food for the large community, and in times of famine they provided food for the people of the surrounding valleys as well. The arts were also cultivated, and students were instructed in philosophy and theology, Latin and Irish, history and scripture. In the monastery's scriptorium, monks spent long hours copying out books of the Bible and other authors and embellishing the pages with exquisite ornamentation. It was the Irish equivalent of a university.

At the centre of the monastery's life lay the work of prayer. Each day the hours of the Divine Office were chanted together by the monks. Each day the sacrifice of the Mass was offered for the souls of the living and the dead. The spiritual father of the monastery was the abbot, who ruled over the monks and other members of the community. The valley was also the seat of the Bishop of Glendalough, whose diocese included most of the modern counties of Wicklow and Dublin, apart from the city of Dublin itself.

For twelve days young Laurence explored this marvellous new world, overwhelmed by the multitude of impressions, deeply touched by the kindness that surrounded him. Then his father arrived to take him home.

❦ ❦ ❦

It is not hard to imagine the emotion and joy of the meeting between father and son. The two years had been almost as much of an ordeal for Maurice as for Laurence. In his gratitude, he turned to the bishop who had helped to secure the exchange of hostages and offered to send one of his sons to be educated in the monastery. Which son? It didn't really matter, said Maurice. And he airily suggested that the easiest way of deciding would be for the bishop to draw lots.

There was more than one reason for the bishop to be taken aback at this suggestion. The clear implication was that the son was being sent to Glendalough not just to learn reading and writing but to take religious vows and become a member of the community. Pulling straws or tossing coins seemed a strange way of deciding which of the sons had a religious vocation.

Furthermore, it could well be that Maurice intended that the son in question should in due course become Abbot of Glendalough. A monastery of the size of Glendalough had extensive revenues from its crops and cattle. When an abbot died, there was usually considerable jockeying by the local chieftains in an effort to get a member of their own family appointed as the new abbot. In the past, they had sometimes used bribery or violence to get their way. It was by no means rare for a member of a ruling family who was not even a monk to be elected abbot. He would then enjoy the revenues of the monastery while totally ignoring its spiritual function.

All these were good reasons for the bishop to show a distinct lack of enthusiasm at Maurice's offer. He was unexpectedly rescued from his dilemma by Laurence himself. 'My Lord,' he said, 'there is no need to cast lots. I am willing to be educated in clerical doctrine.' Then he added in a burst of childish candour, 'Anyhow, I am afraid of being put in chains again by the king.'

Maurice could not hide a smile, while the bishop and other priests present openly showed their joy. In his short time among them, the boy had impressed them favourably and they were glad that he was choosing to stay not at his father's bidding but of his own free will. Maurice then took Laurence's right hand in his and formally handed him over to the bishop for the service of the Church and of St Kevin.

Maurice returned home, leaving Laurence with the bishop, who took him into his own house and looked after him as long as he lived. Despite his late start, the boy showed great industry and aptitude at his studies. Beginning with reading and writing, he went on to Latin, theology, scripture and philosophy. Pages from two of the books used in the monastery of Glendalough at that time are preserved in the British Library and give some idea of the course of studies that Laurence was required to follow. One is *The Art of Grammar*, a Latin primer by Clement Scotus, an Irish scholar who became head of the Emperor Charlemagne's famous school in Aachen about the year 800. The other is entitled *The Abacus*, and is an extract from a continental textbook of the period on mathematics.

The old writers give us little information about Laurence's early years as a monk. The only incident that interrupted the tranquillity of his life was the death of the bishop who had proved such a good friend to him in his time of need and whom he mourned as a second father. Apart from this, he followed the normal routine of study, work and prayer. His reputation for holiness and wisdom grew among the community and he began to be spoken about as a possible future abbot. No mention is made of his ordination to the priesthood and we are not certain when this took place.

In the year 1153 the Abbot of Glendalough died. His name was Dúnlaing O'Cahill and he was a member of the O'Cahill family who wielded considerable political power in the area. Since the beginning of the century, five abbots had ruled the monastery and four of them were O'Cahills. The other one was an O'Toole. The scene was set once again for a battle between the two families to see which of them would provide the next abbot, and the word battle is no mere metaphor. The single O'Toole abbot had been killed by his enemies in 1127. Glendalough was a prize worth fighting for and killing for.

Laurence was twenty-five years of age when the abbot died. He was very young for the position but by now he had won the respect and affection of most of the monks. In addition, he had the considerable influence of his father Maurice to back him up. There may well have been older monks who had the necessary qualifications for the position but it was not enough in those troubled times to have the necessary qualifications. The right political connections were more important.

The election involved not only the members of the monastic community but all the people who lived in the valley and formed part of the larger community. The result was decisively in favour of Laurence. Despite his youth, there was general satisfaction at the result. The monastery now had an abbot who was not a layman imposed from outside but a monk who had been a member of the community from his boyhood, and who was interested not in feathering his own or his family's nest but in working for the good of souls.

In this way, at the age of twenty-five, Laurence O'Toole became Abbot of Glendalough. He soon proved that his electors had made no mistake. His rule was to be a short one, only about eight years, but it was long enough to make him the greatest Abbot of Glendalough since St Kevin himself.

❧ ❧ ❧

The first few years of Laurence's abbacy were to be a very testing time. The opposition did not die down at once. There was a dangerous conspiracy against his life organised by what the Lives call 'certain noble and well-educated clerics'. These would have been monks and other clergy belonging to the O'Cahill family and their allies, and they were relying on help from their numerous kinsmen to bring about Laurence's death and secure the abbacy for their own candidate. The conspiracy withered away from lack of support. Even those initially opposed to Laurence were quickly won over by his obvious holiness and dedication.

The next problem Laurence had to face was famine. His election as abbot coincided with a period of bad weather and resulting crop failures which lasted for four years. The annals of the time also record an outbreak of cattle disease in Leinster beginning in 1152. Laurence threw all the resources of the monastery into works of relief for the victims of the famine. By careful management and good farming methods, the monks had built up a substantial stock of provisions. In fact, monasteries like Glendalough were used as safe places to store food and valuables even by outsiders, since robbers were likely to be deterred by the sacredness of the place or, failing that, by the number of people guarding it.

Some stories told about Laurence at this time indicate that the peace and order of the monastery did not go far beyond the gatehouse. There was one particularly notorious outlaw in the neighbourhood who belonged to a noble family. He attacked and robbed a group of the abbot's men who were bringing corn and honey to the monastery, leaving a number of them dead. Instead of sending out more of his men to track down the outlaw, Laurence went to the church and prayed for deliverance. Three days later, the man fell into the hands of some of his enemies. Fearing to kill a nobleman, they blinded him instead, but with such brutality that he died anyhow.

A similar story tells of three bandit chiefs who waylaid a group of people travelling to the monastery along the track which is still known today as St Kevin's road. Not only did they rob some and kill others, they also seized and ate the consecrated hosts which the priests in the group were carrying. When they heard about the sacrilege, the abbot and his monks spent a day in the church praying that the malefactors would be brought either to repentance or to justice. A week later, the three leaders fell into the hands of the local king. He hanged two of them at the site of the ambush and the third on top of a rock at the entrance to the monastery, in full view of those entering or leaving the church.

Both these incidents are numbered among Laurence's miracles by the chroniclers, whose criteria for judging the miraculous do not seem to have been very strict. To the modern reader, they are of more interest as a sign of the troubled times he lived in. Some of the robber bands may have been motivated by greed but others were driven by sheer hunger.

In the meantime, Laurence continued with his works of charity and relief. When the foodstocks in the monastery began to run low, he bought food from less badly affected areas. By the time the famine ended, he had run through all the monastery's resources, as well as his own personal inheritance as son of the King of Hy Murray. In addition, he sold his father's treasures, which Maurice had committed to the monastery for safe keeping. Whether Maurice's approval was asked or given is not clear. Certainly, if he had hoped that having a son as Abbot of Glendalough would improve the family finances, he was very much mistaken.

❧ ❧ ❧

In the year 1157 the Bishop of Glendalough, the successor of Laurence's benefactor, resigned his position. Laurence was by now so highly regarded that he was urged by the clergy and people of the diocese to become their new bishop. He refused on the grounds that he had not yet reached the canonical age of thirty. Others would have been less scrupulous and would have leapt at the offer. To be at the same time Abbot and Bishop of Glendalough would mean immense power and influence.

Laurence was not interested in holding two positions. His concern was with the monastic community he had been elected to serve. The worst of the famine was over by this time and the strain on the monastery's resources was coming to an end. Laurence could turn his attention to the building up of the monastery, both physically and spiritually.

The old Lives speak of him as having built churches in Glendalough but do not specify which ones. There are two church ruins there which appear from the style of workmanship to have been built at this time. They are the cathedral and St Saviour's Priory.

The main part of the cathedral was built well before Laurence's abbacy, probably in the tenth century. With a nave thirty feet wide, it must then have been the largest stone church in Ireland. It was further extended in Laurence's time by the addition of a large chancel or sanctuary at the east end. A richly decorated archway inserted in the east wall of the cathedral opened into the new chancel, which almost doubled the length of the building. A decorated doorway on the north side of the old portion was also added at this period. The tiny oratory nearby, known as the Priests' House, was probably built at this time also.

The church known as St Saviour's Priory (that is, the Priory of the Holy Redeemer) dates in its entirety from Laurence's time. There is a tradition to the effect that Laurence built it for a community of Augustinian Canons. Though roofless, it is still in a good state of preservation, and this, the first of Laurence's many churches, is the only one to survive more or less as it was when he knew it.

In many ways it is the loveliest of all the churches of Glendalough, though one of the least visited. To reach it, the visitor crosses the footbridge near the cathedral and turns left to follow the river downstream for about half a mile. The priory church is beautifully situated to the left of the pathway, hidden in a grove of trees on the bank of the river. Perhaps because it is so little visited, the sense of peace and closeness to nature is stronger here than anywhere else in the monastery. The silence is broken only by bird-song, the rustling of the trees and the gentle murmur of the river.

Though considerably smaller than the cathedral, the priory church has the same richness of decoration. Its chancel arch, unlike the cathedral's, survives unbroken, and both the archway and the window openings are adorned with attractive carvings of men and animals. One of the pillars is decorated with a carving of a ship in full sail, an oddly prophetic touch. Though at this point in his life Laurence had probably never even seen a ship, he was to become only too familiar with them in the years to come.

This church, the cathedral and the Priests' House are the only examples in Glendalough of the Romanesque style, which had been introduced into Ireland by the building of Cormac's Chapel in Cashel around the year 1130. They are a sign of Laurence's openness to the new influences coming into the Irish Church from the European mainland.

An even more telling sign of this openness is the tradition that the priory church was built for the Augustinian Canons. The twelfth century was a time of Church reform in Ireland, spearheaded by the two celebrated Archbishops of Armagh, Celsus and St Malachy. Laurence was to become the third of these great reformers. There were many abuses that needed to be corrected: neglect of the sacraments, sexual immorality, infidelity in marriage, disregard of clerical celibacy, plundering of churches and monasteries, appointment of laymen as bishops and abbots. Beginning in 1101, a series of councils was held to root out abuses and to bring the Irish Church closer to the ideal of what the Christian Church should be.

One of the aims of these synods was to renew monastic life in Ireland. New religious orders were introduced into the country, most notably the Cistercians and the Augustinian Canons. Their style of monasticism was very different from the Irish style. Over the centuries, monasteries in Ireland had become more like small towns than religious houses. Glendalough was not so much a community as a community of communities. The different churches may have served the different groups, monks, students, diocesan priests, nuns, lay employees and their wives and families. In contrast, the Cistercian and Augustinian monasteries were tightly organised, with all the monastic buildings grouped around a single church and only monks and novices allowed to live there.

Given the loose structure of the Irish monastery, it was not difficult for Laurence to set up a community of Augustinian Canons in St Saviour's. He may have hoped that their more ordered lifestyle would serve as an example to the other monks and the monastery. He may also have hoped that the monastery as a whole would eventually adopt the rule of the Augustinians. One tradition says that Laurence himself actually lived in St Saviour's and followed their rule.

Whatever his long-term plans for Glendalough may have been, he was not destined to fulfil them. Towards the end of 1161 the Archbishop of Dublin died. Laurence was to be his successor.

CHAPTER THREE

ARCHBISHOP

I t is quite likely that Laurence had never been in Dublin
in his life. To the Irish it was a foreign city, as were the
other sea-ports which the Vikings had founded, Wexford,
Waterford, Cork and Limerick. Of these Dublin was the
largest and richest, though small by modern standards.

The Irish looked on these ports as mere trading posts and
had no conception of the important part taken by towns in
more developed countries. As a result, the Viking towns were
isolated from the mainstream of Irish life and tended to look
more towards England and Scandinavia than towards their
own hinterland. The Vikings in Ireland had begun to accept
Christianity more than a hundred and fifty years before and
there had been a Bishop of Dublin since about 1030. But it is
significant that all the Bishops of Dublin had been of Viking
descent and considered themselves part of the English rather
than the Irish Church. Whenever a new bishop was appointed
to the see of Dublin he went to the Archbishop of Canterbury
for consecration.

Archbishop Grene, also known as Gregory, had been
Bishop of Dublin since 1121, but he became an archbishop
only in 1152 when two new metropolitan sees were instituted
in Ireland. In addition to Armagh and Cashel, the Dioceses
of Dublin and Tuam were raised by the Pope to the rank of

archbishoprics. The four pallia, the signs of an archbishop's authority, were brought by Cardinal Paparo to the Council of Kells in 1152, and the fact that Dublin was included among the four was a sign of its growing importance and of a desire to make it more fully part of the Irish Church. The author of the oldest of the Lives describes what happened next.

> Gregory, Archbishop of Dublin, fell asleep in the Lord. Thereupon, to avoid so important a place being left too long without a bishop, all the nobles of the whole kingdom, both laity and clergy, came together to hold an election. And although there were some who considered themselves to be worthy of the prelacy by reason of their lineage and learning, the Abbot Laurence was the only one considered by the people and clergy to be worthy to take the place of so important a prelate.

This brief account raises many unanswered questions. How was Laurence elected and by whom? Was the election confined to nobility and clergy or did the ordinary people have a say? Does 'the whole kingdom' refer to Dublin or Leinster or Ireland? One thing that can be taken as certain is that Dermot McMurrough was among those who took an active interest in the proceedings. As King of Leinster, he claimed to be overlord of Dublin and was anxious to do everything he could to bring the city under his authority. This claim was resisted by the people of Dublin, who had their own Danish king ruling over them, and it was a cause of permanent tension and frequent warfare between the men of Dublin and the men of Leinster.

The election of a new bishop, the first for forty years, brought these tensions to a head. Dermot was anxious to have his own man as archbishop so as to secure his influence in the city. He wanted an Irishman, better still a Leinsterman, best of all a member of his own family. The Dubliners were slow to oppose his wishes. Dermot was a strong and dangerous ruler who was building up a formidable army in his bid for the high kingship. If the Dubliners elected another Dane, he might easily decide to impose his own candidate by force. This could mean the Leinstermen besieging the city; and even if they did not capture it, they could inflict serious damage and loss of life.

Laurence was the ideal compromise. Strangely enough, he was completely acceptable to Dermot. A reconciliation had been patched up between the McMurroughs and the O'Tooles and cemented, as was so often the case, by a royal wedding. Mór, daughter of Maurice and sister of Laurence, had been given in marriage to Dermot and was now Queen of Leinster. This meant that Dermot would have his own brother-in-law as Archbishop of Dublin, someone he knew to be a man of probity and honour, who would do nothing to undermine his position.

He was equally acceptable to the Dubliners. If they had to have an Irishman, he was the best Irishman there was. He was becoming known throughout Ireland as the greatest Abbot of Glendalough since Kevin himself. Not only had he proved himself a capable administrator, a builder of churches, and a friend of the poor, he was also rumoured to have the miraculous powers of the old Celtic saints. He could heal sickness by laying his hands on the sufferers or merely breathing on them. He could reveal the secrets of the heart and tell penitents of the sins they tried to conceal from him. Moreover, the fact that he was Dermot's brother-in-law would help to bring peace between Dublin and Leinster. But he was no man's catspaw. If he ever had to choose between the interests of Dermot and the interests of Dublin, they believed he would choose Dublin. Events were to prove them right.

It was one thing to elect Laurence, it was another to persuade him to agree. The old Lives describe him as reluctant to accept this high office, because in his humility he felt himself to be unworthy. This is standard hagiography. Lives of saintly bishops at this period invariably describe them as reluctant to accept this high office, because in their humility they felt themselves to be unworthy. But there were other reasons why Laurence might have hesitated. Given the tensions of the situation, he could foresee that he would have to face many trials, though in his worst nightmares he can hardly have imagined just how harrowing they would be. Furthermore, he was a natural contemplative, a man of deep prayer and interior life. He loved Glendalough, he was doing good work there as abbot, he had found peace. Why should he want to become immersed in a world of politics and intrigue? Why should he want to leave?

There was no reason except the feeling that God was calling him. There was a job that had to be done for Dublin and for Ireland and he was the only man who could do it. He gave his consent and was consecrated archbishop in Christ Church Cathedral in Dublin some time in the summer of 1162. It is significant of the new direction he was taking that he did not go to Canterbury for consecration as previous archbishops had done.

The chief consecrator was the Archbishop of Armagh, assisted by two of Dublin's suffragans, the Bishop of Ferns and the Bishop of Leighlin. There is no record of any representative from Canterbury. From now on, the Church in Dublin was to be an integral part of the Irish Church.

❧ ❧ ❧

For the rest of his life, Laurence would sign his name in Latin as *Laurentius Dublinensis*, Laurence of Dublin. It was an honourable title, though the diocese over which he presided was tiny by modern standards. It consisted only of the city of Dublin, which was hardly more than a small town, and a few Viking settlements in the immediate vicinity.

Recent excavations have increased our knowledge of the Viking city of Dublin. Most of the people lived in small houses built of clay and wattles, huddled closely together along narrow streets. These flimsy structures rarely lasted long. They either burnt down, fell down or were knocked down every few years. Diggings have uncovered the remains of many such houses piled one on top of the other. A wall, which may have been a mixture of wood and stone, encircled the city and gave some protection against attackers.

The most important buildings were the churches, dominated by Christ Church Cathedral on the highest point of the hill on which the city stood. The churches and even the cathedral officially known as the Cathedral of the Holy Trinity, were probably built in wood in the Scandinavian style. Some wooden churches built at this period in Norway still survive. They are known as stave-churches and are remarkable for the subtlety of their design, with overlapping roofs and gables, all richly carved and decorated.

The names of some of these Dublin churches are still remembered. The churches dedicated to St Patrick, St Brigid, St Colmcille, St Kevin, St Michael le Pole, were of Irish origin as the names suggest. They had been founded before the Vikings came but were taken over by the newcomers as parish churches and possibly re-built. St Olaf's was called after a Viking saint, and so was St Michan's, the only church on the north side of the Liffey. Near St Michan's was St Mary's Abbey, founded in 1139 for the Benedictines but taken over by the Cistercians eight years later.

The cathedral itself had been founded by Donatus, the first Bishop of Dublin, around the year 1030, by which time the majority of the Viking inhabitants had become Christians. It was served by a college of canons, secular priests of the Diocese of Dublin, and was the centre of the city's religious life. Outside Dublin, its chief claim to fame was a large crucifix, known as the Holy Trinity crucifix, which was credited with miraculous powers and visited by many pilgrims. Gerald of Wales tells a number of stories about it in his book *The Topography of Ireland*.

> There is in Dublin in the Church of the Holy Trinity a cross of most wonderful power. It bears the figure of the Crucified. Not many years before the coming of the English, and during the time of the Ostmen, it opened its hallowed mouth and uttered some words. Many people heard it.
>
> It had happened that a certain citizen had invoked it, and it alone, as the witness and surety of a certain contract. As time went on, the other contracting party denied the agreement and completely and steadfastly refused to return the money which the other had given him according to the terms of the contract. The citizens, more in irony than for any serious reason, declared that they should go in a body to the aforesaid church and hear what the cross would say. The cross being adjured and called to witness, gave testimony to the truth.

The story gives us some sidelights not only on the religion of the Dubliners but on their business dealings. The references to money and agreements and contracting parties are a reminder that in the time of the Ostmen or Vikings there was a flourishing commercial life in the city. Much of this was based on trade with England, Scandinavia and the European mainland. Dublin exported agricultural produce and various manufactured goods, including textiles, gold and silver ornaments, and household articles. The manufacture of combs seems to have been a Dublin speciality. Imports included such items as silk and wine, and there was also a discreditable traffic in slaves. At this time, Dublin was a clearing house for slaves captured in Viking raids in many parts of Europe and even as far away as Africa.

≈ ≈ ≈

This was the city and the people that Laurence found entrusted to his care in the year 1162. It was a city in transition, a pagan city that had become more or less Christian, a Viking city that was in the process of becoming more or less Irish. Many of the Vikings had married Irish women and the two races were beginning to become less distinct. Irish was the language generally spoken in the city and the use of Norse was dying out.

The early Lives of Laurence give a highly unflattering picture of the morals of the Dubliners at that time. One of them describes their response to Laurence's preaching in these terms:

> The citizens refused the nourishment of the Gospel teaching. When he saw that they were persisting in three vices in particular, namely, drunkenness, violence and murder, he was led by the divine spirit to prophesy that these three vices would lead them to their destruction. He foresaw that their drunkenness, which caused the fire of lust, would deserve to be punished by fire, that their violence would deserve to be punished by violence, that their murdering would deserve to be punished by slaughter.

This description need not be taken too literally. The writer is probably indulging in a certain amount of hindsight. There was a tendency in medieval writers to say that any catastrophe was a divine retribution for sin. On this reasoning, since the catastrophe that was shortly to befall Dublin was so severe, the citizens must have been unusually sinful to have deserved it. But the writer is not very informative about the actual sins; the ones he mentions could have been imputed to the citizens of any other city, then or now.

Gerald of Wales is more specific. He singles out the sin of slave-trading as the one which called out loudest for vengeance. According to him, immediately after the destruction of Dublin, a council of all the clergy of Ireland met in Armagh and decided that the sin which had provoked this calamity was the practice of buying English captives from pirates and merchants and selling them into slavery. Those who had made slaves of the English in the past were now being punished by having the roles reversed. The council decreed that all English slaves in Ireland should be given their freedom.

All this lay in the future as Laurence began his new life as Archbishop of Dublin. While the people of his diocese may not have been exceptionally sinful, they were certainly not all saints. There was much to be done, both on the spiritual and material level. He set to work at once.

His first concern was with his own church, Christ Church Cathedral. Europe was now entering the age of the great cathedrals. All over England and the Continent, foundations were being dug and scaffolding erected and massive walls climbing into the sky. Dublin must not be left behind. As the chief city of Ireland, it deserved to have a cathedral that reflected both its faith and its importance. The old Christ Church would have to be replaced.

The physical fabric of the cathedral was important to Laurence but what happened inside it was even more important. One of his first actions was to make sure that the cathedral fulfilled its role as the mother church of the diocese and its chief centre for prayer and worship. The cathedral was staffed at this time by secular canons and it may be that their conduct of services in the church and their lifestyle outside it left something to be desired. At all events, Laurence decided that changes were needed.

As a former monk, his mind naturally turned to the possibility of entrusting the cathedral to the care of a monastic order. The old Irish monastic system of the kind he had known in Glendalough was unsuited to life in the heart of a busy city. The same could be said of the Cistercians, whose rule demanded detachment from the outside world and whose monasteries were normally situated as far away from cities as possible. He opted for the Augustinian Canons, whom he had come to know and respect in St Saviour's in Glendalough.

The Augustinian Canons followed the rule drawn up by St Augustine around the year 400 but they did not come into prominence in the Church until around the year 1050. Their principal monasteries were in France, and from there they spread first to England and then, through the influence of St Malachy, to Ireland. One of the best known of their French monasteries was at Arrouaise, and it was a visit to this house around 1140 that impressed Malachy and made him decide to bring the order to Ireland. Most of the Irish foundations followed the traditions of Arrouaise and in consequence their monks were often called Arroasian Canons.

In many ways, their rule resembled the Cistercian rule. They renounced property, lived in community, and sang the different hours of the Divine Office in common each day. They observed silence in the monastery and fasted from meat all the year round. Unlike the Cistercians, however, they were prepared to undertake the care of cathedrals and other public churches where the good of souls called for it, and to make whatever modifications in the rule were needed to make this possible.

It cannot have been easy for Laurence to persuade the canons of Christ Church to accept the Arroasian way of life, with all the restrictions and austerities that it entailed. It is said that St Malachy himself could not persuade the clergy of Armagh Cathedral to make the change. Where Malachy failed, Laurence succeeded. How he did it we are not told, but it was evidently not easy, as one of the early biographers discreetly admits. 'This task of transforming secular clergy into religious canons,' he writes, 'is so difficult and remarkable that he could not have achieved it without the help of the Holy Spirit, who was his companion all through life.'

After the Dublin canons agreed to become Arroasians, two of their number were sent by Laurence on the long journey to Rome to obtain all the necessary documents from the pope. On their return, the clergy house beside the cathedral was formally constituted an Augustinian monastery and the clergy took vows as Augustinian monks. The cathedral remained in the care of the Augustinian order until the Reformation.

≈ ≈ ≈

Laurence's decision to become an Arroasian monk cannot have surprised those who knew him well. The habit of prayer and contemplation built up over long years in Glendalough was not easily shaken off. The luxurious lifestyle of the medieval prince-bishop was not for him. He needed to pray as he needed to breathe, and his prayer demanded a way of life that was marked by simplicity and self-discipline.

It may have been his own love of the monastic life that finally persuaded the other canons to accept it. Having taken the Arroasian vows, he fulfilled them to the letter. He lived in community with his fellow-monks, wore the habit of the order as they did, and joined them in praying the Divine Office in the cathedral. He took his meals with them in their refectory and ate the same food as they did. From the day he took his vows, he never tasted meat again. He drank wine only when attending official functions, and on these occasions so drowned it with water that it could scarcely be tasted.

His duties as archbishop kept him busy much of the day and made it difficult for him to get time for prayer. It was only at night that he found the peace and quiet he needed. One of the loveliest passages in the Lives describes how Laurence used to rise in the small hours of the morning and go to the cathedral with the others to sing the office of matins and lauds. When the Divine Office was finished and the others were returning to their beds, he would remain on in the church. It was his custom then to make his way to the famous crucifix, of which so many strange stories were told. There, sometimes standing, sometimes sitting, sometimes kneeling, he would recite the Psalms and pour out his soul in fervent prayer to his crucified Lord. One of the monks, who sometimes stayed on after the others had gone, swore that on two or three occasions he heard a conversation taking place between Laurence and the figure on the cross. Finally, as dawn was beginning to break, the archbishop would slip out of the cathedral by the door that led to the little graveyard and walk up and down for a while among the graves, praying for the souls of the faithful departed.

For some reason, that picture of Laurence walking in the graveyard at dawn is the one that remains most sharply etched in the memory. On one side of him is the shadowy mass of the cathedral, on the other the steep slope down to the river from which the early morning mists are already beginning to rise. All around him the city is wrapped in silence and in sleep. Then out beyond the mouth of the Liffey, beyond the bay flanked by Dalkey Island and Howth Head, beyond the restless grey expanse of the Irish Sea, the first streaks of dawn begin to break through the darkness . Somewhere in the city a cock crows and is answered by another. From the huddled wicker huts voices are heard, the sounds of babies crying, fires being raked, water being poured. The silent prayerful figure on the hill watches over the city as it comes alive to face another day.

CHAPTER FOUR

CONTEMPLATIVE

The first years of Laurence's pontificate were a time of hope and opportunity. Neither he nor his people knew what calamities lay ahead and the future looked bright. The horizons of Dublin had begun to open and widen in all directions, mainly through Laurence's influence. For the first time, the town was becoming a part of Ireland, no longer a little foreign enclave but a capital city in the making. At the same time, it was being opened up to new influences from Europe. From the continent came recently founded religious orders, the Cistercians and the Augustinians, bringing with them fresh approaches to philosophy and theology, liturgy and spirituality, music, art and architecture. The city was suddenly coming alive.

Laurence himself, not yet forty years of age, was at the height of his powers. He dominated the city morally, intellectually and even physically. The old writers describe him as *vir magnae et elegantis staturae*, a man tall in stature and handsome in appearance. He was not the ruler of Dublin: it still had its own Viking rulers, who called themselves kings or earls, according as their power grew or lessened. When Laurence first came to Dublin, it was ruled by Ragnall McTorkill, who was succeeded in 1166 by his brother Hasculf, the last Viking ruler of Dublin. But Laurence soon became recognised as the leader and spokesman for the people of the city. To the institutional authority of a medieval bishop, he added the natural authority of a great man.

Soon after his consecration, he started on the church-building programme which was to change the physical fabric of the city. The old Celtic churches, though built of stone, were too small to admit more than a couple of dozen worshippers at a time. The newer Viking churches were larger but they were made of wood and so were at the mercy of the fires that swept so often through the wickerwork city. He began to work on plans for a new cathedral built of stone in a style and on a scale that would rival any of the great churches of Europe. At the same time, he started rebuilding the old Celtic and Viking churches or replacing them with new ones.

During the first few years of his ministry, he is credited with the building of the churches of St Paul, St Andrew, St Nicholas Within and St Mary del Dam. Saint Nicholas Within got its name from the fact that there were two churches dedicated to the saint in Dublin. Saint Nicholas Within was inside the city walls, St Nicholas Without was outside them. Saint Mary del Dam was built beside the Dam Gate which controlled the waters of the River Poddle as it flowed into the Liffey.

A second Arroasian monastery dedicated to All Hallows (All Saints) was founded in the city in 1166 through the generosity of Dermot McMurrough. The paths of the two men continued to cross in strange and usually unpleasant ways all through their lifetimes. As the King of Leinster claiming ultimate sovereignty over Dublin, Dermot was anxious to keep his name and his authority in the public eye. As a notorious slayer of men and burner of monasteries, he was equally anxious to have some good deeds to his credit and some good souls to pray for him after his death. It was a common practice for kings and nobles to endow religious houses in atonement for their misdeeds. Many of the churches and monasteries of the Middle Ages owed their existence less to the piety of princes than to their impiety.

Dermot was also responsible for the founding of the best known convent in Dublin, St Mary de Hogges. It was situated near College Green, which was then called Hoggen Green. It was in this convent that Mór McMurrough, Dermot's long-suffering wife and Laurence's sister, ended her days. As a husband, Dermot was frequently and publicly unfaithful. The whole of Ireland was shocked by his affair with the famous beauty, Dervorgilla, the wife of Tiernan O'Rourke. Her husband had left her in what he thought was safe seclusion on an island in a lake in Meath, while he went off on a military expedition. On his return he found that she had been abducted by McMurrough and was now installed in the royal stronghold in Ferns.

What made the incident so sensational was not the abduction itself – Irish kings were not noted for marital fidelity and the lady seems to have been a willing partner in the escapade - but the fact that Tiernan O'Rourke was the King of Breffni and one of the most powerful rulers in Ireland. The one-eyed warrior king was every bit as violent and ambitious as Dermot himself and swore undying vengeance on the man who had betrayed him.

❦ ❦ ❦

The relationship between Dermot and Laurence was always stormy but never broke down completely. Dermot was a realist and knew that it was important to have Laurence on his side. Laurence was a saint and was prepared to forgive what ordinary mortals would find unforgivable.

A further cause of dissension between the two arose over the appointment of Laurence's successor as Abbot of

Glendalough. The usual dispute broke out between the leading families of the area. Laurence favoured his nephew Thomas, not just on family grounds but because he knew him to be genuinely worthy of the position. He had received Thomas as a young novice and supervised his training as a monk, and he was in a good position to judge his quality. The monks and people of Glendalough agreed with his judgement and were happy to accept him as abbot.

Dermot McMurrough had other plans. He chose one of his own henchmen to be the new abbot and compelled the monks by force to accept him. If he imagined that Laurence would tolerate the situation for the sake of peace, he was mistaken. Laurence could accept a personal affront meekly but he was not prepared to see his beloved monastery made a pawn in a game of politics. The dispute dragged on for a long time but he remained inflexible, refusing to acknowledge the intruder or recognise him as the lawful abbot. Eventually Dermot backed down and the intruder was removed. A proper election was held and Thomas became Abbot of Glendalough.

This happy outcome was a great joy for Laurence. It meant that he could freely return to the place that had meant so much to him, the place that had welcomed him in his darkest hour, given him his vocation and taught him to pray. He began to use Glendalough more and more frequently as a refuge from the pressures of city life and a place of spiritual renewal. He was sure of a welcome from Abbot Thomas, who soon became his closest friend and most trusted adviser.

On his visits to Glendalough, Laurence did not stay in the monastery but in St Kevin's hermitage. There is a certain amount of confusion in the old Lives as to the precise location of this hermitage, and some of them suggest that Laurence used the cave known as St Kevin's Bed as his place of retreat. The so-called Bed is a cavity in the cliff face about thirty feet above the surface of the upper lake, which is supposed to have been carved out by Kevin to serve him as a refuge from the crowds. It is certainly man-made but is now thought to be a prehistoric tomb. It is nowhere more than three feet high and measures less than seven feet from front to back. A man of Laurence's height could only lie in it or crouch with difficulty. To suggest, as some of the Lives do, that he could have spent forty days at a time there is to stretch credulity to breaking point.

What appears to be the oldest of the Lives, transcribed by Dr Maurice Roche from a manuscript in the Arsenal Library in Paris, clears up the confusion. It describes St Kevin's Bed accurately, noting that it could be reached only by rowing across the lake and then climbing a ladder fixed against the cliff face, with one end in the water. It relates how Laurence, following Kevin's example, would often climb up to the cave and there 'keep vigil with the singing of the Psalms'. This apparently means that he would spend the night in prayer in this place which had been made holy by its association with the founder.

The manuscript then goes on to describe the place which became recognised as the archbishop's hermitage and where he was left in undisturbed peace by the monks. This was an area near the cave on a lower level, with grass and trees and a small stream, so overhung by cliffs that the sun never shone on it from October to March and no-one could reach it except by boat. This can only refer to the spot known as Temple-na-Skellig (the Church of the Rock), which is thought to be the site of St Kevin's first settlement in Glendalough.

Temple-na-Skellig is as inaccessible today as it was then. It is a small and narrow grassy area between the foot of the cliffs and the lake shore, with a few little trees and a dry channel which might carry a stream in rainy weather. On it are the remains of a small stone church which certainly dates from well before Laurence's time. Steps lead up from the door of the church to a raised area where layers of ashes and charcoal have been discovered, which are thought to be the burnt remains of the monks' clay and wattle huts. From the other end of the church a series of rough stone steps leads down to a landing place on the edge of the lake. This is the place used by Laurence as a retreat and lyrically described in the Arsenal manuscript.

> Trees with wonderful foliage flourish there, grass of the brightest green grows there. There is also a willow-tree which by a great miracle produces marvellous apples; these are still unripe on St Martin's Feast and almost inedible, and do not fully ripen until Christmas. They remain bitter to the taste and are kept only as a cure for the sick.
>
> There is also a stream of great sweetness springing from the cliff and forever playing with a murmuring sound against the green banks. Fatigued by continuous prayer and fasting, the archbishop would rest beside it, while the sweet singing of the birds enticed him to sleep. In this desert he wore the following clothes: an innermost garment of sackcloth, above this a rough tunic, and above this again a garment of decent cloth. He ate no more than three times a week. He did not stuff himself with choice dainties but fed on bread and water and vegetables and gave thanks for them.
>
> To this place there was no access except by boat. The blessed archbishop would allow no-one to come to him here except his nephew, the aforesaid Abbot Thomas, who would bring to him all matters that concerned his people and take back his replies; or, if the matter was of great importance, would take him back with him.

Laurence's hermitage is part of a great tradition that stretches from the first Christian centuries to the present day. It is significant that the writer describes this grassy and well-watered spot as a 'desert', thus linking it with the earliest monks who went into the Egyptian desert in search of God. The word was taken into the Irish language as *díseart* and was used to describe all those places throughout the country where monks lived in seclusion and solitude. It is still preserved in many Irish placenames in the form of Dysert or Dysart.

Modern spirituality has begun to rediscover the desert. The example of Charles de Foucauld, who spent thirty years in a hermitage in the Sahara, has given rise to brotherhoods and sisterhoods which emphasise the importance of the desert experience in the Christian life. A similar tradition has long existed in Russia and the Russian word for desert, *poustinia*, has given its name to a movement that tries to make the modern city dweller aware of the need to make space for silence and contemplation. In her book *Poustinia,* the Russian-born Catherine de Hueck Doherty describes how she built log huts in the Canadian forest where people could spend a day or two alone, praying and fasting with no companion but a bible. She writes:

> For those of you who go into the poustinia for a day or two, this is the essence of it: to fold the wings of your intellect. In this civilisation of the West everything is sifted through your heads. You are so intellectual, so full of knowledge of all kinds. The poustinia brings you into contact first and foremost with solitude. Secondly it brings you into contact with God. Even if you don't feel anything at all, the fact remains that you have come to have a date with God, a very special rendezvous. You have said to the Lord, 'Lord, I want to take this twenty-four, thirty-six, forty-eight hours out of my busy life

and I want to come to you because I am very tired. The world is not the way you want it, and neither am I. I want to come and rest on your breast as St John the Beloved. That's why I have come to this place.'

For Laurence, the desert was not a flight from responsibility. His days in Glendalough rested him and centred him and strengthened him for his work in Dublin. He could not have been so active if he had been less contemplative.

≈ ≈ ≈

In the rest of Ireland, the armies continued to march to battle. In 1166 a new contender for the high kingship appeared in the West. Roderick (Ruairi) O'Connor, King of Connacht, began to gather allies in a campaign to win the uneasy crown of Ireland. The old high king was defeated and slain and most of the kings of Ireland submitted to Roderick. The only notable resister was the King of Leinster, Dermot McMurrough, who still harboured ambitions of his own.

Roderick led his army into Leinster to crush his last opponent. He found an enthusiastic ally in Tiernan O'Rourke of Breffni. Though Dervorgilla had long ago returned to him, Tiernan's hatred for Dermot had not lessened over the years. Together they penetrated into the heart of Dermot's territory, scattered his outnumbered army and captured his stronghold in Ferns. Dermot barely escaped with his life and took ship for England. Roderick was now undisputed High King of Ireland and he celebrated his triumph by holding the traditional Tailteann Games.

It was a pyrrhic victory. Dermot was not a man to give up easily. He brought his complaints to the King of England, Henry II, and received a sympathetic hearing. Henry ruled England, Wales and much of France, and was by no means averse to the idea of adding Ireland to his dominions. Dermot swore fealty to Henry and in return received an open letter of commendation which was to prove immensely valuable. It read:

> Henry, King of England, Duke of Normandy and Aquitaine, Count of Anjou, greets all his subjects, English, Norman, Welsh and Scots, and all nations under his dominion. When these present letters come to you, know that we have received Dermot, Prince of Leinster, into the bosom of our grace and friendship. Wherefore if anyone from our dominions should wish to assist him to recover his rights as one who has given us homage and fealty, let him know that he has our goodwill and permission to do so.

Armed with this letter, Dermot began looking for allies and found them among the Norman barons and knights of Wales. They were men who were discontented with their lot. Most of them had incurred Henry's disfavour for one reason or another and now found themselves in one of the least desirable parts of his kingdom. They looked greedily at the rich lands of Ireland, a short sea journey away. A hundred years ago their Norman ancestors had conquered England and carved out rich estates for themselves at the expense of the vanquished Saxons. Now was an opportunity to do the same thing for themselves by conquering Ireland. They professed great sympathy for Dermot and promised to give him every support in his attempt to reinstate himself as King of Leinster and make a bid for the high kingship. Their real aim was to use him as a gateway to the conquest of Ireland.

The following year Dermot landed secretly in Ireland and returned to his base in Ferns, where he tried to rally his old supporters. Hearing of his arrival, Roderick and Tiernan again marched against him and again defeated him. They foolishly allowed him to stay on in his ancestral territory on condition that he recoginsed Roderick as high king, gave him one of his sons as a hostage, and paid Tiernan a hundred ounces of gold as compensation for the abduction of Dervorgilla. Dermot agreed to all the conditions, knowing that his new allies across the water were preparing to come to his rescue. The fact that he was condemning his son to death does not seem to have weighed with him in the least.

CHAPTER FIVE

MEDIATOR

No-one in Ireland seems to have had any inkling that a time-bomb was ticking away on the other side of the Channel. Roderick and his trusted ally Tiernan paraded their armies around Ireland, asserting the new high king's authority and adjusting territorial boundaries in their own favour. They were blissfully unaware of the fact that Roderick's reign as high king would very soon be over and that there would never be another.

Laurence's life in Dublin continued as before. As he came to know the city better, he became aware that its wealth was very unequally divided. There was an upper class of merchants who enjoyed a very comfortable lifestyle and a middle class of tradesmen and artisans who were reasonably housed and fed. Below these were people who lived in real poverty, many of them victims of the country's constant warfare and unrest, the old, the disabled, the widows, the orphans. To these Laurence's house was always open. He provided a food service for the poor of the city and even during this time of comparative peace between thirty and sixty people dined in his presence every day. Later the numbers were to increase dramatically.

It was the plight of the homeless children that touched him most deeply. Some were orphans whose parents had died of hunger or disease or been killed in some petty war or other. Others were babies abandoned by mothers too poor to feed and rear them. The old writers tell us that he received these children with a mother's love and took them into his own house to live with him. When their numbers grew too large for him to handle – at one point he had two hundred children depending on him for food and lodging – he boarded them out with the families of workers on the farms owned by the archdiocese.

He also offered hospitality to the traveller and the stranger. A story is told in one of the Lives about a Danish ship which was nearly wrecked off the coast of Connacht. It succeeded in making its way to Dublin, but the unfortunate sailors were attacked by a gang of Dubliners, intent on killing the men and stealing their possessions. Laurence heard about what was happening, rushed to the scene and succeeded in rescuing the sailors. He brought them to his house and cared for them until they were able to continue their voyage. Then he gave them some money, blessed them and sent them on their way.

Stories began to circulate about him, about his generosity, about his ability to read souls, about his power to heal the sick. It was even said that he could raise the dead to life. There was a priest in the city called Galwedius who ministered in St Martin's Church, a good friend and former pupil of the archbishop. He became seriously ill and appeared to be dead, since he showed no sign of life or breath. Some of his friends, however, thought he was in a deep coma and asked for his burial to be postponed. He had been lying in this condition for three days when the archbishop came in, knelt down and prayed over him. The priest immediately sat up, opened his eyes, and asked the onlookers what they were doing there. They told him that they had been preparing to bury him. The priest then said, 'Lord knows my soul was indeed separated from my body. Then, while the angels were disputing for it, I saw blessed Laurence kneeling and praying to the Lord and the Blessed Virgin. Because of his prayers, the merciful Lord ordered my soul to be reunited to my body.' Laurence forbade the priest to tell anyone of the incident, but the story spread and lost nothing in the telling.

The old Lives contain many other stories about Laurence, all of them intended to show that he was possessed of miraculous powers. The people of the Middle Ages loved nothing better than a good miracle story and any saint worth his salt had to have a string of miracles to his name. For this reason, one has to be wary about believing such stories too easily. However, most of the marvels related of Laurence are by no means far-fetched. Indeed, they would not strike the modern reader as being miracles at all. They are stories of answers to prayer, deliverances from danger and disease, uncanny insights into the minds and hearts of others. They are the kind of happenings that one associates with a person of exceptional holiness and deep interior life, whether in the twelfth century or in the twentieth. But taken individually, not one of them would pass the stringent requirements of a modern canonical inquiry.

Laurence was right in trying to dampen the enthusiasm of those who were ready to shout 'Miracle!' at any unusual event. In the incident just related, the priest may only have been in a coma and his recovery when Laurence prayed for him may have been no more than a coincidence. But if it was a coincidence, it was a remarkable one and well worth recording. Other equally striking coincidences occurred during his life and some of them will be described in the pages that follow. They cannot be called miracles but they do suggest a man closely in touch with the world of the spirit, a man whose prayers had a habit of being answered in highly dramatic ways.

Some of these miracle stories have another characteristic which is unattractive to the modern mind, a characteristic which seems to have been peculiar to Ireland. The Irish had a special love for stories in which someone offends a saint and comes to an unpleasant end. We have already seen how the deaths of the robbers in Glendalough were attributed to the power of Laurence's prayers. A similar incident is told of this period in Dublin. One day he heard that a servant of his had been condemned to death for some offence and was about to be executed. Laurence went at once to the place where executions took place, but when the executioner saw him approaching he beheaded the servant before the archbishop could intervene. Seeing this, Laurence called down heavenly vengeance on the executioner. On his way back to the city, the man fell off a bridge, broke his hip and soon afterwards died.

It is difficult to know how to interpret these stories. To the twelfth-century Irish mind, anyone whose maledictions produced such dire results must be a saint. The twentieth-century mind would be tempted to the opposite conclusion, that anyone who makes such maledictions could not possibly be a saint. The most plausible explanation is that these maledictions and curses and calls for divine vengeance were added by later storytellers in a misguided attempt to enhance Laurence's reputation. They were trying to force him into the traditional Celtic mould of the saint with whom you trifled at your peril.

This characteristic of Irish hagiography was noted by Gerald of Wales. In his *Topography of Ireland* he tells a number of these stories to show how even long-dead saints did not take kindly to any form of disrespect. An archer who shot one of the ducks called after St Colman perished miserably. A soldier who jumped over the fire dedicated to St Brigid became lame for the rest of his life. Two of Hugo de Lacy's horses who ate corn stolen from a church dropped dead. He comes to the unkind conclusion:

This seems to me a thing to be noticed that just as the men of this country are during this mortal life more prone to anger and revenge than any other race, so in eternal death the saints of this land that have been elevated by their merits are more vindictive than the saints of any other region.

～ ～ ～

The criticisms of the Irish character made by Gerald of Wales may have been deserved, but he was hardly the man to make them. As a Norman who came to Ireland in the wake of the occupying forces and whose best-known book *The Conquest of Ireland* describes how the occupation came about, he was in no position to adopt a high moral tone. The Norman invaders whose exploits he recounted and whose virtues he extolled were as revolting a collection of cut-throats as have ever disfigured the pages of human history.

In 1169 the first small Norman force landed in Dermot's territory in the south-east of Ireland, and it was joined by another even smaller one in the spring of 1170. The Vikings of Waterford attacked the newcomers but were defeated. Seventy of the Waterford men were captured and against all the rules of war were put to death with extreme barbarity. It was the first act in a deliberate policy of terrorism. 'Let us make the death of these men strike fear into others,' said one of their leaders, 'so that this unruly and rebellious people will shrink from attacking us again.'

In August 1170 the main invasion force landed, two hundred cavalry and one thousand infantry under the command of Richard de Clare, Earl of Strigoil, better known under his nickname of Strongbow. They marched on Waterford, captured the city and embarked on a wholesale massacre of the inhabitants. It was only the arrival of Dermot

McMurrough and his army that put an end to the slaughter. The city was still running with blood as Dermot gave his daughter in marriage to Strongbow, signifying that Strongbow would succeed to his kingdom after his death. Then the two men decided to march immediately on Dublin before the Irish could co-ordinate their forces.

The high king assembled an army and marched to meet them, but Dermot gave him the slip by leading his men through the Wicklow Mountains. On the Feast of St Matthew, 21 September 1170, the people of Dublin were horrified to see the combined forces of Dermot and Strongbow suddenly appearing before their walls. Their city was ill-equipped for a siege, especially against the experienced and heavily armoured Normans. Reports of recent events in Waterford did nothing to strengthen their morale. The whole population was seized by panic.

The only man in Dublin who seems to have kept his head at this point was Laurence. King Hasculf and the other leading citizens could think of little but their plans for escape. The city was surrounded on land but it was still possible to leave by sea. The wealthier Dubliners began to get ships ready and to load all their valuables on to them so that they would be prepared to leave at a moment's notice.

Laurence was determined to stay with his people and he instructed his priests to do the same. He then agreed to enter into negotiations with Dermot and Strongbow to see whether it was possible to come to a peaceful settlement. He met with Dermot's envoy and in the course of three days of hard negotiation managed to hammer out an agreement. The main terms were that the people of Dublin would recognise Dermot as their overlord and would give him thirty of their citizens as hostages to guarantee their loyalty. In return, their city would be spared. These terms were accepted by both Dermot and the Dubliners and the process of selecting the thirty hostages was begun. Not surprisingly, there was a certain reluctance on the part of the Dubliners to volunteer for what could only be regarded as a high-risk occupation. As a former hostage of Dermot McMurrough, Laurence could sympathise with their dilemma.

The news that a peace was about to be concluded was very distasteful to the Normans. They had not come to Ireland for peace but for war. They were not going to let the richest prize in Ireland be taken away from under their very noses. Without the slightest warning, they suddenly attacked the city from two different sides. It was an act of calculated treachery, probably done without Dermot's knowledge. They had the advantage of complete surprise and within minutes the streets of the city were filled with Norman soldiers. The few defenders who tried to resist them were quickly cut down.

Hasculf and the other leading citizens immediately grabbed their remaining valuables and headed for the boats. Gerald of Wales asserts that they tried to bring with them the city's greatest treasure, the miraculous crucifix in Christ Church Cathedral. 'They tried every resource of effort and industry to give effect to this,' he writes, 'but nevertheless the people of the whole city could not move it either by force or skill'. Abandoning the attempt, they hoisted sail and set off to take refuge with their Viking kinsmen in the Isle of Man and the Orkneys.

By this time, the attack on the defenders of the city had turned into a wholesale massacre of the inhabitants. Men, women and children were put to the sword in the streets and houses or drowned in the river. The object was first of all to strike further terror into the people of Ireland, and secondly to amass as much booty as possible while the confusion continued. It is always easier to rob a man when he is dead or a house when it is empty. By accident or design, many of the houses were set on fire and a black pall of smoke began to form over the stricken city.

During those terrible hours, Laurence seemed to be everywhere at once. There are descriptions of him running through the streets, trying to stem the tide of savagery and destruction. One account tells of him making desperate attempts to save innocent victims from death. Another has him defending the churches against arsonists and looters. Yet another describes him taking the still twitching bodies of the slain and carrying them in his own hands for burial. All are agreed that he was many times in danger of losing his own life. The Norman soldiery, crazed by greed and blood-lust, were in no mood to respect him even if they recognised him. When at length he returned home, exhausted and sickened by what he had seen, it was only to find that his own house had been ransacked and the money set aside for feeding the poor had been taken.

≈ ≈ ≈

The following day, a semblance of order returned to the city. The fires were quenched, the wounded cared for, the dead given Christian burial. The Norman knights who had led the attack formally handed over possession of the city to Strongbow. This was a gesture of considerable significance. They had supposedly come to Ireland to restore Dermot to his kingdom, but now instead of yielding their prize to him they gave it to their own leader. The pretence of being Dermot's subjects was being dropped. The Normans were out for themselves.

If Dermot felt aggrieved at this, he did not make an open issue of it. He still needed the help of the Normans for his next move, which was an attack on his deadly enemy, Tiernan O'Rourke. But he must have been aware that he was now in danger of being devoured by the very monster he had called in to help him.

With his usual energy, Laurence set about caring for the survivors. As Archbishop of Dublin, he had control over some of the rich lands that lay to the north and west of the city. He arranged for food to be brought in to feed those who remained alive and provided shelter for those whose homes had been destroyed. The looting of his house meant that for the time being he had no money to share.

The Normans who robbed the archbishop's house had robbed the money of the poor and their action aroused particular anger among the people. If one can believe Gerald of Wales, this anger was shared by no less an authority than the miraculous cross which had refused to be moved from the cathedral. He writes:

> When the city was captured, an archer, among others, offered a penny to the cross, and as he turned to go away, was hit in the back by the penny flung after him immediately. He took it up and offered it to the cross a second time, but the same thing happened, while many people standing about looked on and wondered. Then the archer confessed before all that on that very day he had plundered the residence of the archbishop within the very precincts of that church. A penance was imposed upon him and he returned whatever he had got from the archbishop's residence. He then brought the same penny in great fear and awe for the third time to the cross. This time finally it remained and did not move.

Another concern of Laurence at this time was the repair of the city churches which had been looted and wrecked. Chalices, candlesticks and other sacred ornaments had been taken, along with the vestments and even the missals and other books used in the services. He performed prodigies of improvisation in getting the churches ready once again for divine worship. One of his few consolations was the knowledge that the priests of Dublin had followed his instructions and stayed with their people.

❧ ❧ ❧

Twice more during a period of twelve months, the city of Dublin was besieged. King Hasculf returned in the spring of 1171 with an army of Vikings from the northern isles and made an attempt to recover his kingdom. After a short but savage battle outside the walls of the city, the Vikings were defeated and Hasculf himself captured. He was brought before the Norman leaders and offered his life in return for a ransom. With unexpected courage, he refused to admit defeat. 'This time,' he said, 'we came with a small force but it is only the beginning of our attempts. If my life is spared, this will soon be followed by much greater efforts and very different results.' The Normans had him beheaded on the spot.

Greater efforts did follow and follow quickly. Later that same year a second force came from the Viking isles and thirty of their ships blockaded the Liffey, preventing access to Dublin by sea. At the same time, the High King Roderick O'Connor assembled a large army with the help of most of the kings of Ireland and surrounded the city by land. Roderick's men were encamped at Castleknock and other kings took up positions at Kilmainham, Clontarf and Dalkey. This was a much more serious threat to the Normans in Dublin, who were vastly outnumbered by their opponents.

To add to their problems, the Normans had just lost their only Irish ally, Dermot McMurrough. His attack on Tiernan O'Rourke had not proved very successful, as Tiernan retreated before him and refused to give battle. What was worse, Tiernan persuaded the high king to kill Dermot's hostages, among them his son. All Dermot could do was to loot and burn as many monasteries as he could and then return to Ferns. He was ageing, sick and bitter. All his plans had come to nothing. He had captured Dublin and lost it to his so-called allies. His attempts to become high king had failed. His son was dead through his own fault. His kingdom of Leinster was to be inherited by his odious son-in-law, Strongbow.

Some time around the beginning of May 1171 he died in his castle in Ferns. His name was to be hated and reviled for centuries to come as Diarmait na nGall, Dermot of the Foreigners. But he was genuinely mourned by some of those who knew him best, and the monks and nuns of the religious houses he had founded prayed for his soul. It can hardly be doubted that his great-hearted brother-in-law prayed for him too.

It was a sign of the Normans' sinking fortunes that one of the kings besieging Dublin was Murrough McMurrough, a brother of Dermot's. Another was Laurence's brother, Gillacomgaill O'Toole, who had become King of Hy Murray on the death of their father Maurice. Indeed, Gerald of Wales claims that it was Laurence himself who masterminded the entire operation. He says that it was the archbishop who succeeded in persuading the Irish princes to sink their differences and make a combined attempt to recapture Dublin and expel the invaders. He also says that Laurence wrote letters to the King of the Isle of Man and other Viking leaders and secured their help by promising them a rich financial reward if they were successful. Gerald is the only one of the old writers to make these statements and he offers no evidence for them. Modern historians are uncertain whether to believe him or not. Some of them accept Gerald's statements and portray Laurence as a patriot trying to free his country from foreign domination. Others reject this portrayal and believe that he was by his whole nature a peacemaker, more concerned with stopping bloodshed than with winning wars. Readers must decide for themselves which role best fits in with his character.

If Laurence was responsible for organising the siege against the Normans, it is strange that they should have asked him to act as a mediator on their behalf. The city was now completely cut off by land and by sea and there was only two weeks' supply of food left. A measure of barley was selling for half a mark and a measure of corn for a full mark. Strongbow called a council of his knights and they decided to send Laurence to the high king to seek a peaceful settlement.

Laurence knew better than anyone else the sufferings of the poor people of Dublin in this time of hunger. He agreed to undertake the mission. Accompanied by one of the Normans, he set out for the high king's camp at Castleknock, a strange mixture of tents, huts and cabins, ill-planned and ill-guarded, in striking contrast to the military precision of the Normans. There he met Roderick and put before him the terms offered by the Norman council. Strongbow was willing to recognise and do fealty to Roderick as High King of Ireland. In return, Roderick was to recognise Strongbow as King of Leinster now that Dermot McMurrough was dead. Roderick rejected the terms out of hand. He was willing to leave the Normans in possession of the three towns of Dublin, Waterford and Wexford and nothing more. That was the most he was prepared to offer.

Laurence returned to the city where the Norman knights were still in council, anxiously awaiting his news. When they heard the high king's ultimatum, they decided that their only way of defence was attack. They could hope for no help from England, they had no allies left in Ireland. 'To the Irish we are English,' one of them said, 'and to the English we are Irish. One island hates us much as the other.' They were on their own.

Strongbow immediately led out a picked force of fighting men to attack Roderick's camp, hoping to take him by surprise. The plan succeeded beyond all expectation. They crossed the river and made a detour by Finglas without meeting any difficulty or even, it appears, any outposts or sentries. When they reached the camp, they found the Irish totally unprepared. Many of them were bathing in the river, including the high king. Some of them were killed by the Normans, others fled. Roderick himself had what can only be described as a bare escape. In the abandoned camp, the Normans found huge stocks of meat, corn and meal, enough to keep them supplied for a year. They returned in triumph to the city with their booty.

The siege was over. There was no longer any possibility of starving the Normans out and the Irish lacked the machinery for conducting an assault on the city walls. The kings dismantled their huts and folded their tents and led their armies home. The Viking ships weighed anchor and set their course for the northern islands. Laurence's Dublin had become a Norman city.

CHAPTER SIX

TRAVELLER

It was now the autumn of 1171. Word came from across the Irish Sea that Henry II, King of England, was preparing to visit his new dominion with a large military force. Strange though it may seem, his object was not to subdue the Irish but the Normans. Strongbow had now become altogether too powerful for his liking. He was already claiming to the King of Leinster. Soon he might be claiming to be King of Ireland and breaking all ties with England. Henry felt it was high time to assert his authority.

He landed near Waterford on 17 October with an army of five hundred knights and five thousand soldiers, together with arms, food and other supplies. Among the armaments were a number of movable wooden towers, which could be used for attacking the walls of cities, a clear sign that Henry was ready to use force against the Normans in Dublin and Waterford if the need arose. As he stepped on to Irish soil for the first time, a white hare came out of the undergrowth to welcome him, interpreted by all those present as a sign of good fortune.

The omen did not lie. Henry never had to use his wooden towers. When he entered Waterford city the following day, Strongbow was there to meet him and to proclaim his loyalty. Henry confirmed him in possession of most of Leinster, but reserved the cities of Dublin, Waterford and

Wexford for himself. Then he and his army proceeded by slow stages to Dublin.

During his triumphant progress across the midlands, he received the submission of most of the kings and princes of Ireland. This may seem surprising until it is remembered that the Irish saw him as the only man who had both the desire and the ability to control the Norman aggressors. Even Roderick O'Connor, back in his own kingdom of Connacht, did fealty to the English king through emissaries. The submissions were largely nominal. Henry confirmed the kings in their kingdoms and sent them away with generous gifts. But it was still a recognition of Henry as the ultimate overlord of Ireland and an effective abolition of the Irish high kingship.

Henry arrived in Dublin towards the end of November. He had his men build him a temporary but impressive palace just outside the city walls, near the present-day College Green. Here he prepared to entertain his new Irish vassals on a suitably royal scale. Gerald of Wales describes the scene and adds a story of saintly vengeance for good measure:

> As the Feast of Christmas approached, very many of the princes of that country came to see the palace. There they were filled with admiration at the sumptuous and plentiful fare given at the English table, and at the elegance of the service provided by the attendants. Throughout the great hall, they began to eat the flesh of the crane at the king's invitation, a bird which up to that they had regarded with distaste. Around the same time, some archers in Finglas impiously destroyed the trees in the graveyard which had been planted long before by the hands of the saints and were eaten up by a terrible disease.

It is likely that Laurence was a guest at some of these banquets, and it is tempting to imagine him politely declining the breast of crane while nursing his cup of well-watered wine. We have little definite information of what went on between him and the king during this time, apart from one royal document confirming the possessions of All Hallows Priory and signed as witnesses by both Laurence and Strongbow. It can be taken as certain that their negotiations covered matters of greater moment. Henry had the support of the kings but he needed even more the support of the bishops, and without Laurence he could not hope to obtain it.

Henry had in his possession a document of great importance which he had obtained fifteen years earlier from Pope Adrian IV. This authorised him to enter Ireland for the purpose of strengthening the Christian faith and rooting out abuses, and it commanded the Irish to receive him as their Lord. The pope who had granted the document, called from its first word *Laudabiliter*, had been an Englishman, the only English pope. His successor, Alexander III, was an Italian and was much less favourably disposed towards Henry. Indeed, Henry knew that two papal legates were on their way from Rome and were threatening to excommunicate him and place his kingdom of England under interdict.

The cause of the pope's disfavour was the murder of the Archbishop of Canterbury, Thomas Becket, which had taken place just a year earlier, on 29 December 1170. Thomas had stoutly resisted Henry's attempts to bring the Church under his control and there had been a long feud between the two men. Finally, on Christmas Day, the king gave voice to his frustration in the famous words, 'Who will rid me of this turbulent priest?' Four of his knights left the court, made their way to Canterbury, found the archbishop in the cathedral and killed him on the spot with swords and axes. Afterwards, Henry protested his innocence of any intention to harm the archbishop but he was not widely believed, and it was noticed that he had made little attempt to punish the four knights involved.

For the moment, Henry was safe in Ireland from the pope's anger. That winter was the stormiest in living memory and for several months no ships could cross the Irish Sea. He had a chance to redeem himself by making a start on his promised reform of religious practices in Ireland. When calmer seas returned with the spring, he would have something solid to point to as proof of his good faith, something which would show that he had at heart the good of the Church in general and of the Irish Church in particular. He might persuade the pope to drop all threats of excommunication and to confirm him as overlord of Ireland. The best way of doing this was by calling a council of the Irish Church at the earliest opportunity.

Laurence was at first favourably impressed by the king. Henry was an unpleasant man but an able ruler, who had brought peace to England after decades of civil war. If he was willing to do the same in Ireland, if he was willing to control the Normans, keep peace among the Irish, and help in the work of religious reform, he deserved full co-operation. Laurence was happy to support the planned council and it was arranged that it should meet in Cashel early in 1172.

≈ ≈ ≈

In spite of the continuing bad weather, there was a very full attendance at the council. There was some doubt about the attendance of the Archbishop of Armagh who had grown amiably eccentric in his old age. 'The people regarded him as a saint,' Gerald tells us. 'He took a white cow with him wherever he went and lived only on its milk.' In the event, the winter journey must have proved too much either for the archbishop or for the cow and neither of them appeared.'

The old Lives give us a vivid glimpse of Laurence on his way to the council, a commanding figure on horseback, accompanied by the Bishop of Kildare, the Bishop of Glendalough, the Abbot of Glendalough, and their attendants. It was customary for bishops to be attended by a large retinue, for reasons both of dignity and of protection. Some prelates of the period would travel around their dioceses with an entourage of a hundred or more retainers, and would eat the unfortunate parish priests they visited out of house and home. Laurence did not indulge in pomp on this scale, but he was always careful to maintain the dignity of his position. Even when wearing a hairshirt for penance, he would make sure that his outer garments were appropriate to his rank.

They broke their journey near a small settlement to recite the hours of the Divine Office. As Laurence was dismounting, a man rushed up and said, 'My Lord, your duty is not to ride around proudly with an escort of horsemen, but to implore God's help for the Sick. There is a noblewoman in the church near here who is tormented by an evil spirit and has lost her mind.' Laurence, who may have been slightly nettled by the rebuke, suggested to his companions that one of them might go to the church and pray for the woman. Abbot Thomas refused, as did Bishop Malachy of Kildare, but Bishop Clement of Glendalough agreed to go.

The bishop, described as a big bald man, entered the darkness of the church to be met with a stream of insults. 'You filthy bald-headed whoremonger!' she screamed, 'what have you come here for?' Then she picked up a stone and flung it at him. He retreated hurriedly and told the others what had happened. Laurence, perhaps feeling a little guilty, consented to face the woman himself. He entered the church and was greeted with even fouler insults than his predecessor. He ordered the woman to be tied up and laid his hands on her, marking her with the sign of the cross and giving her blessed water to drink. Then he lay down in front of the altar and prayed with all his heart. After this, he left the church and continued on his journey to Cashel.

The Council was presided over by Christian O'Connery, Bishop of Lismore, who had been appointed Papal Legate for Ireland in 1150. The clergy discussed marriage, funerals, the education of children, and relations between Church and state among other topics. Their final report contained seven decrees, of which the first was a vigorous upholding of the Christian teaching on matrimony, the second provided for the baptism and religious education of the young, and the third ordered the faithful to pay tithes to their parish churches. The next two repudiated certain financial impositions which were being made on churches and clergy, and the last two dealt with the making of wills and Christian burial. It was agreed that the practice of the Church in England was a useful guideline to follow in making the necessary reforms.

The decrees were signed and sealed by the legate on behalf of the pope and approved by the king. In themselves, they contained nothing very new and their effectiveness would depend on the way they were carried out. Still, the clergy returned home with a hopefulness that they had not known for many years. They now had a king ruling over them who was firmly committed to maintaining peace and giving them full support in their work of Christian renewal.

On his way back to Dublin, Laurence stopped at the place where he had encountered the possessed woman. He found her waiting for him by the side of the road, fully restored to herself. She ran to greet him and insisted that he and his companions should spend the night in her house. We are told that as he was warming himself at the fire after dinner, she embraced his feet in a gesture of gratitude and devotion.

≈ ≈ ≈

Towards the end of March the winds began to die down and a ship arrived bringing the king news from the outside world. The news was not good. The legates were in Normandy, threatening to put all of Henry's dominions under interdict unless he could meet them and convince them that he was innocent of Becket's death. Worse still, his eldest son Henry and two of his younger sons were joining in a conspiracy to depose him and divide his territories between them. There was much that he still wanted to do in Ireland but he could stay no longer. Just after dawn on Easter Monday, 16 April 1172, he sailed out of Wexford harbour and by midday he had landed in St David's in Wales. He never saw Ireland again.

His six months in the country had been a remarkable achievement. For the first time that anybody could remember the whole island had been united and at peace. It did not greatly matter that their ruler was a foreigner. It was quite common in those days of shifting dynastic alliances for several countries to be united under the same crown. As long as the rights and customs of a country were respected, the nationality of its ruler was of no great concern. Indeed, the very concept of nationality in the modern sense hardly existed at the time.

It is likely that Henry genuinely wished to bring peace and prosperity to Ireland. It was as much to his advantage as to the Irish people's. But scarcely had the mast of his ship disappeared over the horizon than the Normans resumed their briefly interrupted conquest of the country, pushing south and west and north from their principal base in Dublin. Henry was too occupied with his other problems to check them, even if he had the will to do so. The Irish kings resisted the

Norman inroads with all the force at their command and within a few months the country was once again a trembling sod. One of the first victims of the new offensive was the one-eyed King of Breffni, Tiernan O'Rourke, killed at a peace conference with the Normans in circumstances which even Gerald of Wales finds it difficult to explain away.

All these events touched Laurence very closely. Dublin itself was not again attacked during his lifetime and for the citizens it was a time of comparative peace. But Laurence was now a national figure, greatly in demand as a mediator by all sides. No greater tribute can be paid to him than the fact that he was the one man in Ireland whom everybody trusted. When the Normans had been besieging Dublin, he was the one sent to mediate with them on behalf of the Vikings and Irish in the city. When the Normans in turn were besieged in Dublin by the Irish and Vikings, they turned to him to negotiate terms of peace. It is a sad fact that time and time again his negotiations ended in failure and betrayal but this was not held against him. Irish, Vikings, Normans, all had equal respect for him as a man of total honour and integrity.

During the years that followed, he continued to be called on as a mediator. This often meant travelling across the Irish Sea to the court of Henry II in England. The details of many of these negotiations are now lost, but we know that he was one of these who signed the Treaty of Windsor in 1175 which ended a period of tension between Henry and Roderick O'Connor, who was still surviving as King of Connacht. It is safe to assume that Laurence played a leading part in bringing about this peaceful settlement. Quite a few of the miracle stories told about him give us an insight into the difficulties and dangers facing sea travellers at that time. One story relates how he was travelling to England in a convoy of three ships when a violent storm blew up and threatened the lives of all on board. The sailors came to him and begged him to save them. He knelt down and began to pray and at once the winds dropped and the sea became calm.

Another story concerns the return journey from Henry's court to Ireland. Laurence found himself marooned for a long time in Wales awaiting a favourable wind and had almost run out of money. Nearby there was a new church which had not yet been consecrated because the bishop was away. A hermit who lived in a cell attached to this church had a vision of the Blessed Virgin in which she said she wanted Laurence to perform the consecration.

Laurence refused at first because it was not his diocese, but he was told that the vision had warned that he would not get a favourable wind until he did as he was asked. He agreed then to carry out the rite of consecration. There is a charming description of him in the church during the ceremony singing the preface of the Mass with his face turned towards the east, in accordance with the rubrics. Suddenly and dramatically, the east window begins to rattle. He realises that the wind has changed and is blowing fair for Ireland. He finishes Mass, has a hasty meal and rushes down to the quayside. The ship sets sail and a strong easterly wind brings him swiftly and safely home.

❧ ❧ ❧

The transformation of Dublin into a Norman city went on relentlessly. Settlers were brought in from England, mainly Bristol, and many of the former inhabitants were forced to leave to make way for them. These Viking Dubliners settled on the north side of the river in an area which became known as Ostmanstown (now Oxmanstown). North or south of the river, they remained part of Laurence's flock and their spiritual needs were cared for by St Michan's parish church.

The English newcomers were also part of his flock and represented the Dublin of the future. In the space of ten years, Dublin had changed from a Viking city to an Irish city and then to an Anglo-Norman city. He, the first Irish bishop, was also to be the last for many centuries. His successors for the next four hundred years would all be drawn from Norman stock.

Laurence retained the respect of the Norman rulers of Dublin to the end of his life. He rebuked where rebuke was necessary but he did not seek confrontation for its own sake. He was willing to co-operate with them in so far as it was for the good of the people and one area in which he worked happily with them was in the building of churches and especially of the longed-for new cathedral.

The Normans in Ireland were indefatigable builders. They built churches and monasteries of a size the country had never seen before. Since they built them to make reparation for their sins, it was appropriate that they should have built them on the grand scale. Laurence accepted their munificence because It was for the good of souls, but he may well have reflected that the wealth they were pouring into church buildings was only a fraction of what they had stolen from the Irish. But, as is usual in human affairs, the greater the crime the less likely it is to be punished. The poor archer who stole money from Laurence's house and offered a penny to the cross in Christ Church had it flung back at him. The rich baron who plundered a monastery in Meath and endowed a church in Dublin met with nothing but praise for his generosity. It is not difficult to draw an analogy with our own day, when a petty shoplifter goes to jail and a swindling millionaire retires to a luxury home in the Bahamas.

The most lasting physical mark that Laurence left on the city was the new Christ Church Cathedral. Old records indicate that he and Strongbow worked closely together on the project but it is not certain how much of the work was done during their lifetimes. Strongbow himself died in 1176 and was given an elaborate funeral with Laurence officiating. We are told that he was buried in the cathedral within sight of the celebrated cross. This certainly refers to the old cathedral, which must have continued to exist while the new one rose beside it and gradually absorbed it piece by piece. For reasons both of finance and technology, the building of a medieval cathedral normally extended over generations or even centuries. The crypt of the present cathedral is the only part that Laurence is likely to have seen even partially completed.

Other churches and religious houses were founded during these years. The churches of St John, St Michael and St Werburgh date from around this time. In 1174 Strongbow founded a priory in Kilmainham for the Knights Hospitallers, with an almshouse and hospital for the poor. In 1177 Henry II founded the Abbey of St Thomas the Martyr in Donore for the Augustinian Canons, commemorating the murdered Becket who had been recently canonised. Laurence's part in these Norman foundations is not known, but he was certainly as heavily involved in raising funds for church buildings as any of his modern successors. One last sea story has to be told, to illustrate the point.

Laurence was making another of his journeys to England and had already boarded the ship when a number of wealthy Dublin Citizens arrived with valuable merchandise and joined him for the voyage. They had heard about his ability to calm a storm with a prayer, and they felt that they and their belongings were perfectly safe as long as they were in his company. They were evidently men who did not easily part with their worldly goods and it may be that they had shown a certain reluctance in the past to contribute to the building of the new cathedral. If so, the last laugh was to be with Laurence.

They were sailing peacefully along when suddenly a violent storm arose from nowhere and the ship was in imminent danger of going down. The citizens rushed in a body to Laurence and begged him to pray for their safety. 'Have no fear,' he answered. 'Not one of you will be lost. Listen to my advice and appease the anger of God with pious gifts. As you know, we are building a church in Dublin in his honour and in honour of the Blessed Virgin his mother. My advice is that you help to finish it by giving goods to him from whom you received all goods. And then, I promise you in God's name, the sea will grow calm and there will be no further danger to yourselves and your possessions.'

The citizens lost no time in fetching their most valuable possessions and presenting them to the archbishop. When this had been done, he offered up a short prayer which pierced the heavens and brought an end to the storm. The winds died down and the sea grew calm again. The chronicler ends by saying that all gave praise to God and to his holy bishop. It is possible that their praise was tempered by the feeling that this time they had met more than their match.

CHAPTER SEVEN

LEGATE

The journeys back and forth between Ireland and England became more burdensome as the years passed. The difficulties of travel were trial enough. The reception that awaited Laurence in England was an even greater trial.

Relations between him and Henry II became steadily worse. The euphoria of the royal visit to Ireland had completely vanished. Every meeting between the two raked up old grievances and added new ones. The very presence of Laurence was a reproach to the king's conscience, a reminder of hopes betrayed and promises broken. His reaction to the Irish question was the same as that of all succeeding English governments: a peevish wish that it would go away and leave him alone.

By this time Henry had more or less made peace with Pope Alexander III. He did public penance at the tomb of the martyred archbishop in Canterbury Cathedral. In return, the pope confirmed him as Lord of Ireland and called on the Irish kings and bishops to accept him as such. The king did all in his power to ensure that the pope had little idea of the true state of affairs in Ireland.

It was an unwelcome shock to him when he learned that Alexander had decided to call a Council of the whole Church.

The Council, called the Third Lateran Council, was to meet in Rome during Lent 1179. Bishops from all over the world were invited to attend, together with other senior clergy and theologians. Henry was in a dilemma. The Irish bishops were likely to inform the pope of the way he had been carrying out, or failing to carry out, his stewardship in Ireland. But if he prevented them from going, it would be an offence to the pope and an indication to the whole of Europe that he had something to hide.

He decided not to stop the Irish bishops from attending the Council but ordered them to come to see him on their way through England. Six bishops from Ireland made the journey to Rome, the Archbishop of Dublin, the Archbishop of Tuam, and the Bishops of Limerick, Waterford, Killaloe and Lismore. Shortly after Christmas the six arrived in England and made their way to Windsor, where Henry was residing at the time. There they were received in audience by the king, who proved to be in a belligerent mood. Before dismissing them, he forced them to swear an oath on the Gospels that they would do nothing in Rome which would in any way injure his rights in Ireland. They left his court like chastened schoolboys and made their way to the Channel ports.

Four of the six embarked at Boseham, near Chichester. Laurence and the Bishop of Limerick left from Dover. The road to Dover went through Canterbury and it is very probably on this occasion that one of the strangest of the miracle stories took place. According to the old writers, Laurence came to the cathedral in Canterbury to ask for the intercession of St Thomas and spend the night in prayer before the martyr's tomb. The monks received him with all due honour and asked him to celebrate Mass in the cathedral on the following morning. As he was on his way to the altar in full pontifical vestments, he was suddenly attacked by a man who emerged from the congregation carrying a large club and struck him on the head with all the force at his command. Laurence fell to the ground bleeding profusely and was thought by the onlookers to be dead. After a little while, however, he raised his head and asked them to bring him some water. He blessed the water and told them to bathe the wound in his head with it. The blood stopped flowing, he got up, went to the altar and said Mass as though nothing had happened.

The incident happened before a large crowd of witnesses and is one of the best attested of these miracle stories. Whether the healing was miraculous or not, it was certainly extraordinary enough to be long remembered. What is of perhaps greater interest, is the reason behind the attack. The old chroniclers say that the attacker was a madman, who believed he was doing Laurence a favour by allowing him to share in Becket's martyrdom. He was arrested and condemned to be hanged on the king's orders, but was allowed to live when Laurence interceded for him. The possibility cannot be ruled out, however, that this was an attempt to remove the bishop who was increasingly becoming a thorn in Henry's side. Whether he was acting with Henry's knowledge or not, the assassin might have felt he was doing him a service and could hope for a suitable reward.

≈ ≈ ≈

The Irish bishops arrived in Rome about the beginning of March. The Council opened in the Basilica of St John Lateran on the fifth of the month with a ceremony of great pomp and splendour. The pope presided on an elevated throne and was surrounded by the college of cardinals and the prefects, senators and consuls of Rome. The Fathers of the Council numbered almost a thousand and included 302 bishops. In addition to the six from Ireland, there were four from England, two from Wales and one from Scotland. Scotland also sent two bishops elect, who were consecrated by the pope during the Council. One of these was so poor that he had only a single horse for the journey to Rome. The other, even poorer, walked all the way.

Much of the work of the Council was concerned with patching up a recent schism which had been caused by the anti-pope Callistus III. There were also a number of decrees issued, dealing mainly with matters of Church discipline. One of them rebuked clergy for undue display and limited a bishop's retinue to thirty horsemen and an archbishop's to fifty, a decree which can only have been of academic interest to the horseless bishop from Scotland. Others dealt with the elections of popes and bishops, the education of poor clerics and the provision of asylums for lepers.

As often happens on such occasions, what happened outside the Council chamber was of as much importance as what happened inside. It provided a unique opportunity for bishops from all over Christendom to meet one another, compare notes, share problems and solutions. There was no language problem as everyone present spoke Latin. For Laurence in particular it was a heaven-sent opportunity to give the pope a firsthand account of the situation of the Church in Ireland.

Laurence was not inhibited by his oath to do nothing that would damage the king's rights in Ireland. He had no intention of damaging the king's rights in Ireland or anywhere else. But his conception of the king's rights was very different from Henrys. For Laurence the king had no right to do wrong. The king had no right to allow his barons to kill and burn and loot to destroy towns and plunder monasteries, to convert property intended for the work of the Church to their own selfish use. The king had the duty to protect his subjects from violence and injustice, and the duty to further the Church's work in so far as lay in his power. In Laurence's eyes the king was abusing his rights and neglecting his duties.

Alexander, who was nearing the end of his long reign, was one of the ablest popes of the Middle Ages. An experienced administrator and a shrewd judge of men, he found himself deeply impressed by Laurence. There were limits to his power to improve the Irish situation, but within those limits he did all he could. From those meetings with Alexander in the Lateran Palace, Laurence brought away three important documents. The first related to his own Diocese of Dublin. It placed the diocese under the protection of the pope and confirmed to Laurence and his successors all the possessions, rights and privileges of the see. The second was similar to the first except that it concerned the Diocese of Glendalough, which had always been so close to Laurence's heart. The third appointed Laurence to be the new Papal Legate for Ireland.

When all is said and done, a document is still only a number of words written on a page, no matter how many impressive seals and signatures it may bear. Rome was a long way from Ireland and the pope looked very small from that distance. Yet the knowledge that Laurence was now the pope's ambassador and that his diocese and all its buildings and lands were under the pope's special protection would certainly have some restraining effect on Henry and his Norman subjects.

There was also the continuing work of reform in the Irish Church. This would now be Laurence's special concern in his capacity as papal legate. His ministry was no longer confined to the Diocese of Dublin and its suffragan sees. The whole of Ireland was his diocese.

※ ※ ※

Laurence returned from the Council in the late summer of 1179. He started immediately on his new duties as papal legate. As a result of his time in Rome, he had many plans for the renewal of the Irish Church and he decided to summon a Council to see how they could be put into effect. The Council did not meet in Dublin but in Clonfert in Connacht and was attended only by the bishops of the west and north of Ireland.

The reasons for this are not entirely clear. It may be that Laurence intended to hold a second council later on for the south and east, perhaps in Cashel, perhaps in Dublin itself. But his choice of Clonfert for this first meeting was of some significance. It lay in the territory of Roderick O'Connor, still the most powerful of the native Irish kings. It was attended by the Bishops of Connacht and the North, the two areas where the power of the Normans was at its weakest. This was to be a truly Irish council, free from foreign influences, providing Irish solutions for Irish problems.

The decrees of the Council survive only in a somewhat garbled summary. Their main object was to free the Church from improper lay interference so that it could do its proper work. The problem was by no means confined to Ireland. Laurence's talks with fellow bishops in Rome showed him that every country had similar difficulties. In Ireland one of the worst abuses was the number of dioceses which were actually ruled by laymen whose only interest was in siphoning off as much as possible of the diocesan resources for their own personal gain. Previous Irish councils had denounced this abuse without having much effect. Laurence's Council went further. It named seven laymen who held bishoprics and deposed them from their sees. This was a convincing indication of Laurence's firmness and indeed of his courage, given the violence often surrounding episcopal appointments.

The Council also passed a decree ruling that sons of bishops and priests should not be admitted to Holy Orders. This was intended to encourage a stricter observance of the law of celibacy by the clergy and to root out the abuse by which bishoprics and other benefices had been passed down from father to son as if by hereditary right. The Archbishop of Tuam, one of those present at the Council, was himself the grandson and greatgrandson of previous Abbots or Archbishops of Tuam.

Laurence had a deep personal conviction of the value of celibacy in the priest's life. It was one of the values being promoted by Church reformers throughout Europe in the twelfth century and it had been a principal concern of the Second Lateran Council in 1139. The custom that priests should not marry grew up gradually in the Church and was inspired by the teaching on the excellence of virginity found in the Gospels and the Letters of St Paul. The celibate priest showed his total commitment to the values of the Gospel and freed himself from earthly ties so as to serve God more single-heartedly.

There is no doubt that some advocates of celibacy overstated their case and seemed to suggest that human sexuality was in itself something imperfect and even sinful. This never formed part of the official teaching of the Church, which emphasised the sacramental nature of Christian marriage. The celibate priest did not give up marriage as something evil. He gave up one good for the sake of another and higher good. The Third Lateran Council, which Laurence had attended, included in its decrees a condemnation of the Albigensian heresy, which held that sexual relationships and even the human body itself were intrinsically evil.

During his brief period as legate, Laurence showed great firmness in dealing with priests who were living in concubinage. It would appear that these priests were subject to some form of suspension or excommunication from which only the pope could absolve them. When he came back to Ireland as legate, Laurence enjoyed the same powers as the pope and could absolve these men, but he was very reluctant to do so. On one occasion, we are told, he sent forty priests to Rome for absolution.

At first sight, this seems a very harsh way of dealing with human weakness. Some of Laurence's defenders have suggested that these priests were Norman carpet-baggers whom he was trying to remove from his diocese but the explanation is somewhat far-fetched. More likely, he saw that a mere form of absolution would not change anything. The men would go back to the same homes and the same partners and inevitably slip back into the same way of life. What they needed was not absolution but conversion. They needed to make a decisive and costly break with their past. The long pilgrimage to Rome was to be both the sign of their sincerity and the means of their conversion.

～ ～ ～

The winter of 1179–80, the last winter of Laurence's life, brought unusually severe weather to Ireland. The old annalists use the phrase 'the snow of destruction' to describe the icy spell that held the whole country in its grip. It is likely that the preceding summer and autumn had also been wet and cold. The bad weather and the continuing unrest in the country meant that there were shortages of food and fuel and clothing, bringing great distress to the poor, especially in the city of Dublin.

Laurence once again took on the responsibility of providing food and shelter for those in need. It was his last effort on behalf of the poor in Dublin and his greatest. For many years he had been providing in his house a daily meal for the destitute and a shelter for homeless children. He continued these services during this terrible winter for numbers that increased every day. Different Lives give different statistics. One of them says that at the height of the scarcity he was feeding eight hundred people a day.

The number of children to be cared for was also growing. Many mothers, unable to feed their children, brought them to Laurence to be cared for. Some of them left their babies in the street outside his house or in other places where he was to pass, knowing that he would see them and take pity on them and bring them home.

Eventually he had to face the fact that he was coming to the end of his resources. He simply did not have the food to feed so many. He knew, however, that food was in plentiful supply in England and he had built up many contacts there over the years. He chartered a ship, fitted it out, filled it with those who were suffering most from hunger and cold, gave them what money he could afford, and sent them to England to be cared for until the worse was over. It is pleasing to see England appearing for once in a favourable light in his life, and it reminds us that the Norman invaders were by no means representative of the English people. Indeed, the English had suffered as much as the Irish during their own Norman conquest a hundred years earlier. If their sufferings were shorter, it was only because their subjugation was quicker and more complete.

He devised a different stratagem to help his homeless children. He selected the older boys, gave each of them a wooden cross to carry, and sent them out into the countryside to look for food. As they went from farm to farm, the country people gave them all they could spare from their own poverty, because of their love and respect for the great archbishop whose cross they were carrying.

Spring came, the spring of 1180, and Laurence was off on his travels once more. He had to make yet another journey to the court of the English king. Neither he nor his beloved Dubliners knew that they would never see one another again.

CHAPTER EIGHT

SAINT

L aurence's last journey was one more attempt to bring peace to his troubled country. Five years earlier he had helped to negotiate the Treaty of Windsor between Henry and Roderick. Now the treaty was beginning to unravel. A serious disagreement, described in the Lives as 'a great storm of dissension', had arisen between the two monarchs on the question of a tribute or tax which the Irish king was supposed to pay to the English one. Roderick asked Laurence to go to England to make peace, and gave him his own son to take with him. The youth was to be offered to the English king as a hostage.

A meeting with Henry was probably the last thing that Laurence wanted at this point in time. The king by now had heard all about Laurence's activities in Rome, which he regarded as hostile and treacherous. No doubt he was also getting reports from his Norman subjects in Ireland, complaining about the new legate's increasingly independent line of action. His Council in Clonfert was serving as a rallying point for the Irish, a sign that the people of Ireland were perfectly capable of reforming their Church without the help of the English king. His documents giving papal protection to the Dioceses of Dublin and Glendalough were making it difficult for the Norman magnates to indulge in their favourite pastime of acquiring lands belonging to churches and monasteries. Laurence was fifty-two years of age and had been legate for less than a year. The appointment was normally for life. If he had done so much damage in a year, what might he do in ten? Some way must be found of neutralising him.

When Laurence arrived in England, he found that the king was holding court in Oxford, and made his way there. Gerald of Wales says it was through 'zeal for his people' that he had obtained the Roman documents which the king found so offensive. It was the same zeal for his people that brought him to Oxford to plead once again for peace and to brave the wrath of a man notorious for his suspicious temperament and violent outbursts of rage. Gerald, who knew Henry personally, describes him in these words:

> Henry the Second, King of the English, had reddish hair, grey eyes, a large round head, eyes whose greyness became glassy and suffused with red when he was angry, a fiery complexion, a husky voice, a neck that bent forward from his shoulders, a broad chest, powerful arms, a fleshy body and a huge belly, which came from nature rather than from gluttony … He was a very eloquent prince, except when he was perturbed in mind or seized by anger.

At the meeting in Oxford, Laurence had an opportunity to see Henry at his angriest, the grey eyes glazed and bloodshot, the husky voice almost incoherent with rage. All Laurence's pleas on behalf of Roderick were rejected. All his attempts at explanation were swept aside. There must have been moments when he feared for his liberty, even for his life, and not without good reason. But Henry had not forgotten the international furore over the death of Becket and the humiliating public penance he had been forced to undergo in front of the martyr's shrine. Laurence was not only an archbishop, he was a papal legate as well. There were limits to what Henry dared to do.

Laurence was not killed or imprisoned, but what happened to him was almost as bad. The meeting ended with Henry forbidding him to return to Dublin or Ireland. To ensure that his orders were carried out, he issued an edict to all ports in England and Wales, forbidding any ship's captain to provide the archbishop with transport to Ireland. Laurence left the king's audience-chamber as a prisoner in all but name, shut out from the city to which he had been appointed archbishop and the country to which he had been appointed legate.

≈ ≈ ≈

We have little information about Laurence's activity during the next few months. It would probably be truer to speak of his inactivity than his activity. Much of the time was spent in the monastery of Abingdon, a Benedictine monastery not far from Oxford. He was marooned there in a kind of no-man's-land while the fretful monarch roamed around his dominions, first in England and then across the Channel in his dukedom of Normandy.

The weeks passed into months and there was no sign of the king returning to England. Laurence was becoming more and more impatient at the idleness which was being forced upon him. Finally, he could endure it no longer. He was unable to return to Ireland but there was no ban on his travelling to France. He decided to cross over to Normandy, find the king and make one more effort to resolve the situation. Perhaps by now the king's anger might have cooled and it would be possible to make him listen to reason.

It was late October or early November when Laurence and his companions sailed from Dover and crossed the Channel to the port of Wissant. The group accompanying him included the son of the King of Connacht, a cleric by the name of David who was the lad's tutor, Laurence's chaplain Nehemiah, and one of his Augustinian confrères from Dublin named John. No doubt there were also a number of laymen to look after the horses and offer protection, but the chronicler remarks that his retinue was small for an archbishop, and more in keeping with his sanctity than with his office.

They had scarcely landed when Laurence became ill with fever and was forced to rest for three days. On the fourth day, the fever was no better but Laurence once again became impatient and insisted on continuing his journey towards the town of Le Mans, where the king was holding court at the time.

It soon became apparent that he was growing weaker. Even though he tried his best to disguise it from the others, he himself felt that his end was near. Still he refused to rest, and as they journeyed on through the rich countryside, he would ask the names of the various churches and monasteries they passed. It seemed to his companions that he was waiting to hear one name, a name already known to him as the place where he was to die.

They came at length to a hill from which they could see not far away a town and a large church. Once again Laurence stopped people passing by on the road and asked them the name of the town and the church. They told him the town was the town of Eu, and he was now entering Normandy, the territory of the King of England. He then pointed to the largest of the town's churches and asked its name. They said it was the Church of the Blessed Virgin Mary, under the care of the Augustinian Canons of the Order of St Victor. This was a sister congregation of the Arroasian Canons to which Laurence himself belonged.

It was the answer he had been awaiting. 'This is my resting place for ever,' he said, 'here shall I dwell, for I have chosen it.' The words were taken from Psalm 131. The hill where he paused and said those words is now marked by a cross and the little Chapel of St Laurence.

They continued on into the town of Eu and made their way to the Church of Our Lady. Laurence entered the church and spent a little time in prayer, commending himself to the Lord and to his Blessed Mother. Meanwhile, his companions went to the nearby abbey to inform the monks of his arrival and to ask for help. The abbot, Osbert by name, hastened to offer the hospitality of the monastery to his distinguished guest, and Laurence was brought into the house where he was to die. It was Monday, 10 November 1180.

As soon as he arrived, he was put to bed by the monks. He asked the abbot to hear his confession. The abbot did so and then brought him Holy Communion. It was decided that David, the prince's tutor, should go on ahead to the king's court to inform him of the archbishop's condition and repeat his plea for a peaceful settlement of the dispute.

The following day Laurence's condition worsened and by Wednesday he was obviously close to death, though his mind was still perfectly clear. He asked the abbot and the monks to come to his bedside and requested that they would admit him as a member of their community, which they willingly agreed to. Then he asked to be given the sacrament of the sick and was anointed with the holy oil on the eyes, ears, nose, lips, hands and feet. As a priest, he had already been anointed on the palms of his hands in ordination, so this time it was the backs of his hands that received the oil. The suggestion was made to him that he should make a will but he answered, 'The Lord knows that I have not a penny under the sun.' All his personal money had been spent long ago and, in accordance with his vow of poverty, any money he now had was the property either of the diocese or the order.

On Thursday he was still alive, anxiously awaiting news from David. It was as though he was reluctant to die until he had heard the king's response. David returned before evening and was brought to Laurence's bedside. The news was good. Perhaps moved by the archbishop's illness, the king had agreed to the peace terms proposed by Roderick. He had also lifted the ban on Laurence's return to Ireland, and though this was too late to be of practical importance it was still welcome as a sign of goodwill. We are told that Laurence showed his joy and rested his head for a little while against David's breast in a gesture of gratitude and affection.

On Thursday night and all during Friday the fever was intense. As he tossed and turned, he repeated the words of the Psalms in Latin, especially the words of Psalm 56, 'Have mercy on me, O God, have mercy, for in you my soul puts its trust.' Then in a kind of delirium, he began to speak in Irish. One of the old Lives gives a moving description of these, his last words:

> Since charity never fails, and since he so greatly loved those he had left desolate in Ireland, he began to lament passionately over this people who remained his tender concern up to the end. The expression on his face and the words he spoke in the Irish language bore sad witness to his great distress of mind.
>
> When the brothers from the monastery who were present asked what he was saying and why his face and his spirits seemed to have changed, the members of his household were too distressed to answer. At length one of them yielded to their entreaties. He was John the Arroasian Canon, who was mentioned earlier.

With many tears, he translated the words of the saint, saying: 'He is lamenting over the desolation of his people and over the loss of souls. He is saying, Alas, you foolish and senseless people, what will you do now? Who will cure your grievances? Who will be your healer? And many other things in the same vein.'

They remained at his bedside all through the day. As night drew on his last strength deserted him. He died just before midnight on Friday, 14 November 1180.

≈ ≈ ≈

It is said that on that same night a man by the name of Vincent living in Dublin had a dream. He dreamt that he was in Christ Church Cathedral and that he saw the high altar falling down upon him and breaking into fragments. The next morning he told everyone of his dream and said that their archbishop must have passed away. It was later discovered that the archbishop had died on the same night and at the same hour as the dream had taken place.

On this night also people who lived in the neighbourhood of Eu saw a great brightness suddenly appear above the monastery and light up the whole sky, so that they thought at first the monastery had been struck by lightning and set on fire. This was seen and testified to by many people.

These two stories marked the beginning of the cult of Laurence in Dublin and in Eu. He was buried in Eu and, though his heart was sent back to Christ Church where it still remains, it was at his tomb in Eu that the movement for his canonisation began. The place soon became a centre of pilgrimage for the whole north of France and many miracles of healing were said to have taken place at his intercession.

The monks at Eu were immensely proud of their holy man and it was they rather than the Diocese of Dublin that were most active in working to have him declared a saint. In fact, there was a certain lack of enthusiasm in official circles in Dublin. Henry appointed an Anglo-Norman, John Comyn, to succeed Laurence and the Norman influence soon became completely dominant in the Church in Dublin. These Norman clerics found Laurence just a little embarrassing. It was difficult to tell the story of his life and work and sufferings without referring to the fact that his life was grieved, his work doubled and his sufferings largely caused by the actions of the Norman invaders. While they may not have tried to kill devotion to Laurence, they certainly made no great attempts to keep it alive.

In Eu there were no such inhibitions. A steady stream of pilgrims came to the archbishop's tomb and the stream became a torrent after the instantaneous cure of a boy who had been deaf and dumb from birth. The fact that the boy had previously been brought to St Thomas's tomb in Canterbury without avail added to Laurence's lustre. The abbey church soon became too small to hold the crowds and the monks replaced it with the magnificent basilica which still stands over his tomb.

At the same time, the monks were making requests to Rome to have their saint canonised. A number of petitions over the years were unsuccessful for one reason or another and the monks began to lose heart. It was not until more than forty years after his death that the process really got under way. The then Archbishop of Dublin, the confusingly named Henry of London, collected evidence from surviving witnesses about Laurence's life and sent on the material to Eu. The Abbot of Eu added accounts of the miracles worked at his tomb and brought the whole dossier to Rome. The evidence was accepted and on 5 December 1225 Pope

Honorius III declared Laurence to be a saint. The Bull of Canonisation paid long and elaborate tribute to the new saint's virtues and miracles and ordered his feast to be observed each year on 14 November, the anniversary of his death.

The tribute paid by Gerald of Wales in his description of Laurence's last days was much briefer, a mere four words. Writing less than ten years after his death, he described him as *vir bonus et justus*, a good and just man. But to give at least one Norman his due, those simple words ring truer than all the studied eloquence of the papal document. Rightly or wrongly, Gerald believed that Laurence had stirred up resistance to the Norman invasion and organised the siege of Dublin. Yet in the end he retained only the memory of a good and just man. It is hard to imagine a more genuine tribute. Even those who should have hated him, loved him.

684040746043

'Definitiv[...] [...]. Bullock
has done [...] se of the
personal, the enlightening and the profoundly affecting'   *Gscene*

'A history that digs deep'   *R'n'R Magazine*

'A good starter kit to give a queer teenager who doesn't know anything
ab[...] t all the music that comes before Lady Gaga, or for older queers who
tur[...] d out new music after the second decade of Elton John'   **PopMatters**

'A [...] cinating book, a fascinating subject – oh to have a look around [Darryl's]
re[...] d collection!'   **Grant Stott on the Janice Forsyth Show,
BBC Radio Scotland**

'It [...] 10 secret that the LBGT community has played a huge role in the
de[...] lopment of Western music, but Bullock's book excavates and gives a
fu[...] ccount of the artists whose sexual identities were blunted or erased
co[...] letely in the face of extreme prejudice'   **Thrillist**

'B[...] ock leaves no stone unturned in this crucial part of LGBT culture'
Men 24 Magazine

'R[...] vers the lost history of music made by, and for, the LGBTQ commu-
nit[...] Bullock touches on artists as unalike and historically far-flung as the
flar[...] oyant ragtime-era pianist Tony Jackson… [whose music] gave hope to
fea[...] l, isolated LGBTQ kids'   *Publishers Weekly*

'Ut[...] ly engrossing… a deep and dense history, examining in rich detail the
pr[...] ssion of artists and their musical expression'
Dublin University Observer

'Fo[...] vs the history of LGBT music, discovering well-known artists and
a h[...] number of forgotten, often-declared LGBT performers who were
act[...] far before Stonewall'   **XXZ Magazine**

'T[...] bly the best title I've seen all year; a chronicle of the lives and impact
of [...] BT artists, both well-known and obscure. Really fascinating'
Wilde on My Side

'Bullock's sensational reference guide uncovers a lot of fascinating and unfa-
miliar queer history and shares it in an entertaining and breezy style'
Shelf Awareness